The Employer's Guide to Obamacare

Kaya Bromley, JD, MSW is leading a movement to teach business owners how they can turn implementing the Affordable Care Act (ACA) into profit centers.

Any time this country faces a challenge, some people become paralyzed with fear and anger while others find opportunity for innovation and profit. The ACA presents a unique opportunity for business owners to strategize and innovate while their competition sits on the sidelines.

As an attorney and speaker, Kaya has helped hundreds of organizations design and implement plans for ACA compliance. More importantly, she has helped organizations move beyond mere compliance to strategic thinking and cutting edge solutions. Kaya is a recognized business strategist and the President/Founder of Your Obamacare Advisors. Among those she has advised on the ACA are farm labor contractors, car dealerships, law firms, insurance companies, brokers, PEOs, staffing firms, and restaurants including franchisees of McDonald's, Burger King, El Pollo Loco, Five Guys, Marco's Pizza, Tropical Smoothie and Carl's Jr. Kaya has also been recognized for her work in helping to develop a state of the art, ACA compliant program, FreedomCare Benefits.

The Employer's Guide to Obamacare

The Employer's Guide to Obamacare

What Profitable Business Owners Know About the Affordable Care Act

By Kaya Bromley, JD, MSW
America's Leading Business Strategist on the Affordable Care Act

The Employers Guide to Obamacare
What Profitable Business Owners Know About the Affordable Care Act

First Edition

ISBN: 978-1502351517

Your Obamacare Advisors
930 Tahoe Blvd., Suite 802-460
Incline Village, Nevada 89451

Kaya@YourObamacareAdvisors.com

www.YourObamacareAdvisors.com
www.KayaBromley.com

For Web and Katy, whose housekeeping skills kept us from living in complete squalor while I spent every waking hour researching and writing this book.

Acknowledgements

THANK YOU! THANK YOU! THANK YOU!

My clients. Thank you for your courage in facing this law head on, for participating in my think tank sessions and for answering my endless questions.

My family. Thank you Web and Katy for your love and support and for the sacrifices you both made while I was writing this book.

My colleagues. Thank you for wading into these unknown waters with me and spending countless hours debating and arguing with me before conceding to my point of view.

My coach. Thank you Stephanie, for seeing this book complete before I even saw it as a possibility, then for keeping me accountable every time I felt like giving up on it.

FreedomCare Benefits. Finally, a huge thank you to the folks at FreedomCare Benefits for leading the way in ACA innovation and for giving me the honor of advising you and working with you to develop a unique, state of the art, ACA compliant program.

Legal Disclaimers

This Book Is Not:

1. A Substitute For Legal Advice
2. A Substitute For Tax Advice
3. Political
4. B.S.
5. An Excuse To Do Nothing
6. A Reason To Panic
7. The same old stuff you've been reading
8. Confusing
9. Filled with information you do not need
10. The Final Word On The ACA

IRS CIRCULAR 230 DISCLOSURE:Pursuant to requirements imposed by the Internal Revenue Service, any tax advice contained in this book is not intended to be used, and cannot be used, for purposes of avoiding penalties imposed under the United States Internal Revenue Code or promoting, marketing or recommending to another person any tax-related matter.

"When everything seems to be going against you, remember that the airplane takes off against the wind, not with it."

Henry Ford

Contents

Preface

If I were you, I would be wondering why I should spend my valuable time reading this book. What is special about it?

I will cut to the chase. Here are the top 10 reasons why my book is worth your time:

1. **I Read The Law.** I have actually read the ACA and the commentary, understood it and can explain it in plain English.

2. **Legal Perspective.** I am a recognized attorney who has been practicing law both in law firms and as in-house counsel for companies for over 12 years.

3. **Client Perspective**. I have examined this law from numerous clients' perspectives and I have clients from nearly every major fast food brand (franchisees of McDonalds, Burger King, Wendy's, Carl's Jr., El Pollo Loco, Marco's Pizza, 5 Guys Pizza, Subway) plus a variety of different industries (insurance, hospitality, farm labor, automotive, staffing, legal, financial, real estate). This gives me a unique perspective on various applications of the law and allows me to give advice that is universally applicable. My experience comes from things that have actually

happened; not just theory.

4. **Business Owner Perspective.** I am a business owner and I served as General Counsel for Marco's Pizza for 6 years. Therefore, I also look at the law in terms of how it will impact my own companies' operations and bottom line.

5. **I Understand The Insurance Plan Options**. I have advised several insurance companies on the ACA mandates and strategies and have also helped to develop a unique, ACA compliant self-insurance program.

6. **The Basics.** I don't like to waste space in my brain (or yours) with unimportant facts. This book does not include lots of facts and statistics about the ACA that might be interesting if you are running for office, but that won't help you run your business.

7. **No Politics.** I have no political agenda and I don't care about your political views (in a good way). Therefore, the only things you are going to get from me are the facts and my educated advice.

8. **I Am An Innovator.** I live my life by a philosophy of legally breaking the rules once I learn the game. My approach is to teach you the rules of the ACA game and then to teach you the tricks most people will miss.

9. **I Am An Idealist**. We achieve the most when we have to fight for it. When everything is sunshine and rainbows, we have no reason to change, to evolve or to grow. Idealists like me just see the opportunity in the midst of the struggle. The ACA is a struggle, but it is filled with opportunity if you are looking for it.

10. **I Take My Own Advice.** I did such a good job summarizing the ACA in this book that I use it as my resource guide when I need to look something up on the ACA.

I learned one of the most valuable lessons of my life at summer camp in northern Michigan when I was 13 years old. The counselors had tied lots of ropes between 2 trees such that they formed a giant spider web. My team of 8 people had to get every person from one side of the spider web to the other, and each person had to pass through one of the holes without touching the ropes. If anyone touched a rope, everyone had to go back to the beginning and start over. To avoid us taking the easy way out and sending everyone through the big hole at the bottom, they made a rule that each hole could only be used one time.

Since some of the holes in the spider web were as high as five feet in the air, it took teamwork and strategizing to not only figure out how to get everyone through, but also to figure out how to make sure the last person was going to be able to get through without help. At first, I thought the task was impossible and suggested we skip this event and get on to swimming.

Luckily, my teammates started giving their ideas and soon we started passing people through the holes. We quickly learned which holes we wanted to save for the last few people and which ones required someone strong to throw and someone strong to catch. Many times, I was sure that we were stuck and that there was no way to figure it out. Each time, someone else or I came up with another idea and we got a little bit further.

Every time someone touched the rope and we had to start over, we reassessed our strategy and started over. At one point, because most of our teammates were on the other side, some of us had to take running jumps through the holes and our teammates on the other side had to catch us. After nearly 2 hours and starting over about 50 times, we got every single person through the spider web.

The lesson I learned that has fueled me throughout my career and businesses is this:

There is always more than one solution to every problem.

Any time I feel stuck in my life or my business, I rest in the fact that even though I may not see the solution, a solution always exists. Sometimes I may need to ask others for help, take a step back and reassess the situation or take a running jump and hope to hell something or someone catches me on the other side. I have found that as long as I hold true to this core belief, I always find a solution.

I wrote my first book, "The Obamacare Handbook" as a simple summary of the law for employers. It was so useful that I began handing it out to my clients and was using it myself when I needed to look something up. What changed in my practice and why I chose to write this book is that I have seen first hand that there is more than one way to deal with the ACA. I wrote this book to share my findings with you.

In my practice, I not only advise employers, I am increasingly being asked to advise entrepreneurs and businesses who are coming up with innovative services or programs to help employers deal with the ACA. I advise them on how to comply with the ACA and on any other laws that might come into play.

My favorite one was several years ago when a group of business owners, lawyers and insurance guys invited me to a series of meetings to discuss what they were going to do about the ACA in their own businesses. After months of bouncing ideas off of each other and examining different options, we developed a completely unique solution that is guaranteed to be ACA compliant. We quickly realized that our solution could also be shared with other employers across the country and therefore decided to create FreedomCare Benefits. Best of all, the program we designed completely removes the documentation nightmare that I believe is going to be the most difficult and costly pitfall for employers to navigate. FreedomCare Benefits is an example of the innovation I am seeing. It is business owners coming up with solutions for business owners.

While it is easy to think there are no good solutions for employers dealing with the ACA, this could not be further from the truth. There are not only solutions; there are great solutions. Some of the tools I have seen have always existed, but either we did not think we needed them or they seemed like too much work. Other tools are being created out of necessity. Overall, the ACA has caused all of us to look at things differently because the rules have changed.

The reason I do what I do is that I am an agent of change. From my first career in Organizational Social Work where I analyzed public policy and advocated for intelligent community organization to my current career as a legal advisor and business strategist, I see that we are in a constantly evolving society. Change is only scary when we deny it or resist it. When we search for opportunities and face it head on, change can be exciting and fun.

The purpose of this book is to give business owners hope. Healthcare reform is changing business in this country daily. My job is to help business owners stay one step ahead of it. In this book, I have shared my secrets and strategies for helping my clients see the light in a seemingly dark tunnel. My approach has worked for them and I know it will work for you.

At Your Service,
Kaya Bromley, JD, MSW
President/CEO
Your Obamacare Advisors
www.YourObamacareAdvisors.com

When the wind rises,
some people build walls,
others build windmills.

Chinese Proverb

Introduction

$130 Billion Dollars!

The Congressional Budget Office has estimated that the US Government will collect $130 billion dollars in penalties and excise taxes from companies failing to comply with the Affordable Care Act (ACA) over the next 10 years.[1] While they can't fund a month of government spending with that kind of change, it sure will help pay for the thousands of new IRS agents that have been hired to perform ACA audits.

In case you are one of the business owners who thinks, "It probably won't happen to me," think again. It is through penalties paid by employers like you that this law will receive a large portion of its funding. If you are a large employer, you could be assessed penalties by the IRS any time one of your employees qualifies for a subsidy on the insurance exchange. Even if you are offering insurance! Not only that, it will take a minimum of 18 months before you even find out that you are being assessed a penalty. Then if you try to dispute it, you will have to prove your case to the IRS. If you do not have proper documentation to prove your position, you

[1] The Congressional Budget Office (CBO), *Budget and Economic Outlook* for 2014–2024.

could face penalties as high as $2,000 per employee per year, $3,000 per employee per year or $100 per employee per day.

Do I have your attention yet?

The bad news is that the ACA is one of the most confusing and complicated laws US employers have ever had to face. The worse news is that every time you think you have a handle on it, it changes. The reality is that it is the law has been upheld by the Supreme Court as constitutional and if you are an employer in the US you have to comply.

Is there any good news? Believe it or not, there is good news. While I am the first to admit the law can be brutally difficult to understand, it is not impossible. CPA's, attorneys and insurance brokers are doing a great job of teaching their clients about the basics. With a bit of effort, it is possible to educate yourself enough to avoid the obvious pitfalls.

I am not, however, in the practice of simply helping business owners avoid the obvious pitfalls. That is just step one. I am in the business of helping my clients become masters of the law so that they move beyond mere *compliance* to *strategy*.

Compliance is merely "the action or fact of complying with a wish or command."[2] While *strategy*

---

[2] Citation (Def. 1) in Oxford Dictionaries, Retrieved March 25, 2014 from http://www.oxforddictionaries.com

means "a plan of action or policy designed to achieve a major or overall aim,"[3] every employer's overall aim should be to be as profitable as possible. Well, what if I told you that I have met business owners who have learned how to comply with the law in ways that allow them to be even more profitable than they were before the ACA? How can this be?

It is a little known fact that more people became millionaires during the Great Depression than at any other time in this country's history. While the majority of people were panicking about the crashing stock market, the strategic thinkers were finding the opportunities to make money, mostly in real estate. It is the struggle that forced them to think in new and different ways.

Similarly, old ways of thinking and buying insurance are not going to cut it in the new world of health care reform. The profitable business owners are going to be the ones who reassess their options and find the opportunities the majority of people miss. In order to be able to identify the opportunities, you have to first understand the landscape.

In this book I lay out in very easy to understand English the basics of the law. Many of the ACA presenters I have heard leave the audience confused and frustrated. It is usually because they are giving too much technical information and failing to give

[3] IBID (Def. 1), Retrieved March 25, 2014.

only the basic points that a business owner needs to know. While the law and the regulations explaining the law do indeed cover a lot of paper (tens of thousands to be precise), there are really only a very few things you need to know as a business owner.

In the next few chapters, I break down the entire ACA into four easy to understand buckets (using the acronym "LIPS"… catchy, I know).

L is for **L**arge Employer
I is for **I**nsurance
P is for **P**enalties
S is for **S**trategy

This organization gives you a framework within which to understand the fundamentals that businesses must consider in developing an overall strategic plan. There are then a finite number of concepts that fall within each bucket and for each bucket I include a list of the potential pitfalls, opportunities and timelines for implementation.

No matter what you have done so far, my advice to you is to start planning now. When we wait until the last minute to do our taxes we waste all that time feeling stressed, we forget things we might have reported and we lose money. Waiting until the last minute to deal with the ACA will have the same result. Only, more is at stake than ever before. The time of sitting on the sidelines waiting to see if it will go away has passed. Now it is time to face the ACA head on and get ready.

I assure you that if you use the tool and tips in this book, you will be well on your way to becoming ACA compliant. Better yet, you will have the tools you need to join many of my clients who have figured out how to turn implementing Obamacare in to a profit center.

Chapter 1:

THE BIG PICTURE

If you can't explain it simply,
you don't understand it well enough.
~Albert Einstein

Far Left and far Right extremists have been making over-the-top or end-of-the-world claims about the ACA for years. On one side, we hear Pollyanna stories about how the ACA is the greatest thing since sliced bread. On the other side, we hear that it is going to be our country's undoing, or worse, that it will lead to death panels and gun control. The reality is that the reason politicians and talk show personalities are resorting to fear mongering is because they often don't know what the heck they are talking about. Much of what I read and hear about the ACA has very little to do with the facts. And as Herman Melville once said, "Ignorance is the parent of fear."

The purpose of this book is to lift you out of the unproductive political quagmire and into a rational discussion about what the law actually means to you as an Employer. Like you, I have my own opinions about health care reform. People often try to pull me into political debates about it, but my response is always the same. I might share my political views over a glass of vino in my backyard, but overall I find the political debates to be a useless distraction from businesses getting prepared to deal with it.

While the ACA is a politically charged topic, this is not a political book. Whether or not you believe in the law or those who passed the law, it has been upheld as constitutional by the US Supreme Court and we are stuck with it. To make matters worse, it is constantly changing so you can't just learn it once. You have to learn it and stay current as it twists and turns. In this book, I am only going to deal with the facts, what the facts mean to your business and what you can and should be doing about it.

How Is Anyone Supposed To Figure This Out?

I hear this question quite a bit these days. It is usually followed by choice expletives about our Commander-in-Chief, pontifications about the end of 'business' as we know it in America and worst of all, a complete misunderstanding about what the law actually says.

The text of the law is around 1,000 pages long and the volumes of guidance explaining how the law will be implemented are too numerous to count and growing every month. A Google search of the term "Obamacare" or "Affordable Care Act" returns tens of millions of hits. Business owners who are really serious about figuring all of it out would have to shut their doors for a few months to read even a fraction of the information out there. And even if they read it, it is not likely that they would understand it without a law degree. Every few sentences of the actual statute references code sections from other statutes that you would have to look up and understand in order to comprehend the context of the sentence you are reading. Much of it is written in a complex form of legalese that is nearly impossible for ordinary people and even most lawyers to understand.

Thus, the only option for most Americans is to get their ACA education from the media or from right or left wing crazies all of which are mass distributing misinformation, half-truths and confusion. On one side of the street you hear stories of doom and gloom. On the other, you hear promises of deliverance to the Promised Land. The truth, of course, lies somewhere in the middle.

While political discourse is important in order for responsible citizenry to stay involved and aware of government and public policy, there comes a time when the political mudslinging distracts from what is really going on. For the past several years, I have watched business owners sit on the sidelines complaining about what is happening. Although in reality, most of them have no clue what is actually happening or how it is going to impact their businesses. They are grumbling about some tidbit of misinformation that is not even the real problem while their competition, many of whom are my clients, are getting prepared and taking measures to make sure they are not going to get stuck paying exorbitant penalties.

In this book, I am not going to attempt to explain every minute detail of the Law. Those books already exist and quite frankly confused me as much as they will confuse you. The purpose of this book is to give you, a business owner, the fundamentals you need in order to plan for your business. The more you familiarize yourself with the basics, the more you will be ready to start thinking strategically.

How Does This Book Teach Strategy?

Consider when you first started driving a car. If you were like me, your earliest driving experiences focused on staying in your lane, not hitting the car in front of you and remembering to follow the traffic signals. At the beginning, you had to consciously think about the traffic rules to make sure you did not get a ticket or worse, crash your dad's Crowne Victoria. As adults, being in the passenger seat with a new driver reminds us of how scary it was to enter the highway for the first time and what a pain in the *you know what* it was to parallel park before our cars were equipped with rear video monitors.

For those of you who will claim you were always a spectacular driver let me assure you; you were not. In fact, it is precisely because we know that new drivers lack the skill to keep themselves safe driving 55 MPH surrounded by 2 tons of steel that we scare the bejesus out of our kids while they are learning to drive. We scream at them to slow down, turn off the radio and double check their blind spot. Sure, we lie to them and tell them that it is not that we don't trust them; it is that we don't trust the other people on the road. The truth is that we know darn well that they do not yet have the skill and experience to avoid being distracted or making amateur mistakes.

After years of driving, however, things change. The rules become so ingrained in our heads that we don't even think about them anymore. It is second nature to switch on our signal before turning or before changing lanes (well, some of us anyway). And once we had the basic skills down, we got more strategic in our driving. We learned how to time our speed and our turns to avoid the traffic lights. We figured out which roads to take to avoid traffic in certain intersections at specific times of the day. I know I am not the only one who times my lane changes perfectly just before my lane ends to avoid getting behind a semi truck or behind that idiot who keeps letting people like me get in front of him.

The same thing is true in everything we do as human beings. Compare a tee ball player who is just learning to throw a baseball and hold a glove to a major league pitcher who throws the ball in a variety of different ways, each of which is carefully calculated to have a slightly different velocity, trajectory, movement, hand position, wrist position and arm angle. By changing the position of one finger a few millimeters one way or the other the pitcher completely changes the trajectory of the ball making it harder for the batter to hit it. He no longer thinks about the way the coach taught him to hold the ball in little league, but that foundational knowledge was critical to him being able to now have the ability to play strategically rather than just trying to play by the rules.

We have all had experiences like this even if we are not conscious of them. Those of us who have been married for a number of years learned the "rules" that make our spouses tick. After a few years, we now wield the knowledge of which buttons to push that would result in us sleeping on the couch and which ones to press to get breakfast in bed. It is gaining the knowledge and what we do with that knowledge that allows us to control our destiny and success. Life is more interesting and rewarding for all of us when we are the master of our game rather than simply following a set of mundane rules hoping we don't screw up.

For businesses implementing the ACA, today is the day for you to learn the rules of the game. I promise you, it is not going to be as painful as you think. It is, however, the building block for everything you will do in your business related to healthcare reform in the coming years. This law is one of the most complex and onerous laws employers have had to face since President Roosevelt signed the Social Security Act into law in 1935. The requirements placed on employers by the ACA are so complex and the penalties for noncompliance so massive, that no business can afford to ignore it (although many are).

At first, you will be like a new driver who is carefully focusing on learning the rules and avoiding the penalties. With some practice and following the advice in this book however, you will soon be like the pro baseball player and able to change the trajectory and profitability of your entire business just by making miniscule tweaks here and there. Not only that, you will be better able to maneuver new curveballs that will undoubtedly be thrown at you as this law continues to develop and change.

My clients are finding ways to turn 'implementing Obamacare' into new profit centers for their companies.

Sounds too good to be true? Think again. I have a client who has already saved his company nearly $500,000 by taking strategic steps to implement his new ACA compliant health care plan. He began following the law when it was first passed in 2010 and has diligently educated himself on the mandates ever since. Because he understands the basics of the law so well, we were able to come up with ideas for his workforce and payroll that no one had even thought of yet. Our meetings looked less like your typical attorney-client meeting and more like brainstorming sessions where we poured over spreadsheets and insurance quotes.

I have two other clients who have decided to stay away from traditional insurance programs altogether. One is on track to save over $600,000 this year as compared to what it would have paid using traditional insurance. Because they are using a specialized financial vehicle to fund their health care, they are looking at writing off up to $1.2M in their underwriting profits. The other one is actually going to make money by implementing a low cost ACA compliant program and passing on the fee to its subcontractors. The fee is still lower than what traditional insurance would have cost both of them. My clients are finding ways to turn 'implementing Obamacare' into new profit centers for their companies.

The reason this level of planning and strategizing was possible for these two clients is because they have long since mastered the basics. Even if the law changes, which given the history of ACA implementation is a statistical certainty, these business owners will be able to quickly adapt. There is no magic to it. If they can do it, so can you.

Can't I Just Hire Someone To Do This For Me?

I would like to paint you a picture of unicorns and rainbows, but unfortunately the answer to this question is a great big **NO**. Can you hire someone to do your pushups for you? (Hint… see the quote in the box for your answer.)

The problem with simply hiring someone to advise you is that no one understands your business like you do. The insurance industry has done a fantastic job of hiring top lawyers and holding informational webinars to educate their clients. Law firms and CPA firms have also provided massive amounts of valuable information that has helped shape what we understand about the ACA.

> **"You can't hire someone to do your push-ups for you."**
>
> **~Jim Rohn**

Here is the problem: Your insurance broker may have a vested interest in selling you his particular insurance product whether it is the best solution for you or not. Your attorney may give you superb counsel on the law but may have no clue how to run a business. Your CPA, who understands the numbers may have no concept of how his advice impacts employee morale, which directly impacts your bottom line. You get the idea.

Many of the people I have encountered are only seeking ACA advice from one expert. While they are in a better position than those of you who are not seeking any advice at all, seeking advice from a single expert from one discipline is sort of like hiring an electrician to build your house. You will end up with some kickass lighting, but you may have no plumbing and the walls may cave in. Your business has many different facets and you should no more get legal advice from an insurance broker than you should get financial advice from someone who is broke.

The best solution is to consult with different experts who specialize on the different facets of your business – legal, financial, HR, payroll, benefits, etc. The team of experts you build will be instrumental in your success. However, building a team of experts is not enough.

Historians often cite the talented people surrounding Henry Ford as the secret to his success. In fact Henry Ford himself pointed out that he did not bother cluttering up his mind with general knowledge and instead had surrounded himself with an array of educated men who could answer any question he needed answered. He knew how to get any knowledge that he needed and he knew how to use that knowledge to create his plan of action.

However, what makes this story significant is that Henry Ford did not start out relying on other people's knowledge. He first spent decades working as a machinist then as an engineer learning the minutiae of the automotive industry. It was because of his foundational knowledge that he was able to see things in his business that no one else could see. Years down the road when his engineers told him it was impossible to build an eight-cylinder engine block in one piece, Henry Ford told them to build it anyway. Eventually, they did.

The advice given by your expert team may be well meaning and may be dead on within the parameters of their specific specialty. However, no expert is ever going to see everything about your business that you see. Indeed, it is impossible for anyone outside of the organization to have the full perspective of all of the things that go into running your business, your people and your future.

Do not misunderstand me. I am a strong advocate for seeking expert advice. Hell, I am a lawyer and earn my living from people seeking my expert advice. There are circumstances when it makes sense to trust the experts. For example, I think it is a waste of time for a business owner to learn every single nuance of an Operating Agreement. There are a handful of things in the Operating Agreement that the business owner needs to understand and decide. The rest of the document is a bunch of boilerplate that we lawyers typically only change every few years when the law changes or someone smokes up a better form.

You can apply this same concept to learning the ACA. I am not suggesting that you learn every nuance of the law. In fact, I think you are nuts if you try. As onerous and lengthy as the law is, there are only a few things that you need to understand. It is these few things that I am going to teach you in this book.

Ready to start?

The Big Picture

The basic gist of the law as it applies to business can be summed up in a single sentence. It is called "The Employer Mandate" and here it is:

Large Employers must **offer affordable** and **minimum value** health insurance to a **specified percentage*** of their **full-time employees** and their **dependents** or face **penalties**.

* 70% in 2015 and 95% in 2016 and beyond

That's it.

Then why the heck do the webinars by the insurance companies drag on for hours and why are you more confused after the webinars than you were before?

Well, two reasons. First of all, I could write an entire book about each of the words I bolded and underlined above. Each of those words has complex definitions that you must understand in order to follow the law.

The second problem is that there is great information out there, it is just not being taught in a way that makes it understandable for a business owner. I have given numerous presentations with insurance brokers who were very knowledgeable about the law, but only a fellow insurance broker could understand what the heck they were saying. I have also been to presentations where the presenter wants to make sure to impart every last bit of ACA knowledge in his head and ends up giving far more detail than anyone will ever need to know or could ever remember.

The truth is that you do not need to understand every single detail of the law. There are a few basic concepts you need to understand and in this book I have broken them down into four main areas. Beyond that, you need to understand the big picture and you need to understand 'how' to figure out the details.

The diagram on the next page is your basic roadmap to help you understand the Mandate in context of the bigger picture. It shows you how you know if the Mandate applies to you and how you may become subject to penalties. I recommend that you get familiar with this roadmap and refer back to it often because it will make understanding the Employer Mandate much easier.

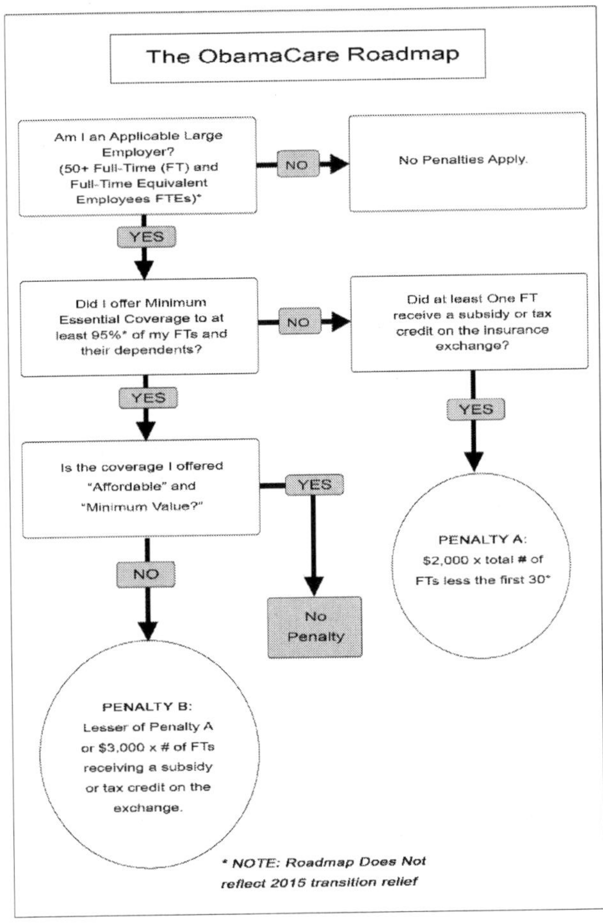
The ObamaCare Roadmap
Am I an Applicable Large Employer? (50+ Full-Time (FT) and Full-Time Equivalent Employees FTEs)*
NO
No Penalties Apply.
YES
Did I offer Minimum Essential Coverage to at least 95%* of my FTs and their dependents?
NO
Did at least One FT receive a subsidy or tax credit on the insurance exchange?
YES
YES
Is the coverage I offered "Affordable" and "Minimum Value?"
YES
No Penalty
NO
PENALTY A:
$2,000 x total # of FTs less the first 30*
PENALTY B:
Lesser of Penalty A or $3,000 x # of FTs receiving a subsidy or tax credit on the exchange.
* NOTE: Roadmap Does Not reflect 2015 transition relief

L.I.P.S.

All law school students use a learning device called "mnemonics" to memorize massive amounts of information for exams. This technique aids in memory retention because it translates information from the original form that is difficult to remember into a new form that is easier for the brain to recall. When I was in law school, my study group partners, Doug and Steve, were especially gifted at coming up with unique mnemonics that were easy for us to recall on test day. Of course, by "unique" I mean dirty and with as many four-letter words as possible. Don't judge. It works.

Alas, Doug and Steve were unavailable to assist me in coming up with something "unique" so the mnemonic I have chosen to help you remember everything you need to know about the ACA is the word **LIPS**. Now that I think about it though, I think Doug and Steve could have created a discussion around this that would have made this mnemonic very "unique."

The following outline is an overview of the entire Employer Mandate. This will give you the big picture and in the next few chapters I will fill in the details.

L is for Large Employer

This covers the basic threshold questions that will help you to understand if and how the law applies to you. Here we look at the following questions:

1. How do I know if I am a Large or Small Employer?
2. What if my partners, family members or I own more than one business?
3. What is the "Controlled Group Analysis?"
4. What special rules apply if I employ Seasonal workers?
5. Who are considered my full-time Employees?
6. What is the Measurement Period, Look-Back Method and Stability Period?

I is for Insurance

Once you determine that you are a Large Employer, the Employer Mandate requires you to offer insurance. The chapter on Insurance will investigate what type of insurance you have to offer.

1. What is "Minimum Essential Coverage?"
2. What does it mean that the insurance offered has to be "Affordable?"
3. What is the "Affordability" safe harbor?
4. What does "Minimum Value" mean?
5. What is the Insurance Exchange and why should I care about it?

P is for Penalties

You will be assessed excise taxes if you are a Large Employer and you either do not offer coverage or the coverage you offer is not the right kind of coverage. I call them "penalties" because if you have to pay them, that is what they will feel like. In the chapter on Penalties we explore the following questions:

1. What is the penalty if I don't offer coverage?

2. What is the penalty if I offer coverage, but it is not the right kind of coverage?
3. What if I am in a controlled group and some of the members offer coverage and others do not?
4. What other penalties do I need to watch out for?
5. How can I avoid paying penalties?
6. Is there ever a time I might opt to pay the penalties?

S is for Strategizing

This is where it gets interesting. This is where we start looking at how you can turn implementing Obamacare into a profit center for your business. There are definite strategic planning opportunities and those of you who take advantage of those opportunities are going to come out on top.

1. What are the planning opportunities?
2. Workforce Strategies?
3. Planning and Pricing Strategies?
4. What kind of records do I need to keep?
5. How can I prepare for an audit?
6. Where do I go for help?

This outline covers everything that will be discussed in this book. It is also everything a business owner needs to understand about the ACA. When you consider the ACA in these terms, it is not so intimidating. Let's begin.

Obamacare in Four Steps		
L	Am I a **Large Employer**?	•50+ FTEs (100+ in 2015) •Who is considered Full-Time •Controlled Group •Seasonal Employee Exception •Measurement Periods Lookback/Stability Method Monthly Measurement Method
I	What type of **Insurance** must I offer?	•What is "Minimum Essential Coverage?" •What is "Affordable?" Safe Harbors •What is "Minimum Value?" •The Insurance Exchange
P	What **Penalties** might I face?	•Penalty A - $2,000 •Penalty B - $3,000 •$100 per employee per day •Cadillac Taxes – 40% tax for plan exceeding certain thresholds •Pay or Play?
S	How can I **Strategize**?	•Workforce Strategies •Documentation and Record Keeping •Planning and Pricing Strategies •Audits •Assistance

Chapter 2:
L is for Large Employer

The secret of getting ahead is getting started.
The secret of getting started is breaking your complex,
overwhelming tasks into smaller manageable tasks,
and then starting on the first one.
~Mark Twain

This Chapter is the first step to building your foundational knowledge of the ACA. It answers the threshold questions you need to ask yourself to determine if the law applies to you and what decisions you can be making to limit your penalty exposure. It also covers the most basic workforce planning concepts you absolutely need to master in order to be prepared for the IRS's reporting requirements.

As I discussed in Chapter One, the Employer Mandate only applies to so-called "Large Employers." Here we are going to look at what a Large Employer is and the different analyses you need to do in your business.

Introduction To The Mandates

The Affordable Care Act includes 2 Mandates:

The **Individual** Mandate
and
The **Employer** Mandate

1. Individual Mandate:

Requires Individuals to have minimum essential coverage or pay a penalty. The penalty is the greater of a flat dollar amount or a percentage of income amounts and is subject to a cap and exemptions.

- **Who is Exempt from the Individual Mandate?**
  - Undocumented immigrants
  - Individuals who are incarcerated
  - Members of an Indian Tribe
  - Individuals or Families whose income is below the threshold to file a tax return ($10K for an individual and $20K for a family)
  - Certain religious groups (these groups have also opted out of social security)

- **How is the Individual Mandate Satisfied?**
  - A qualified plan offered by an employer
  - Medicare
  - Medicaid or CHIP
  - TRICARE
  - Veterans Health Program

- Insurance purchased through an Insurance Exchange

○ **What are the penalties (taxes) for violation of the Individual Mandate?**
- In 2014, the greater of 1% of your annual household income or a minimum of $95 per adult and $47.50 per child (up to $285 for a family);
- In 2015, the greater of 2% of your annual household income or a minimum of $325 per adult and $162.50 per child (up to $975 for a family); and
- In 2016, the greater of 2.5% of your annual household income or a minimum of $695 per adult and $347.50 per child (up to $2,085 for a family).
- After 2016, a percentage of household income adjusted for inflation but no less than $695 per adult and $357.50 per child (up to $2,085 for a family).

○ **Penalties for violation of the Individual Mandate are paid out of an income tax return.**

2. Employer Mandate:

Requires *Large Employers* to offer affordable, minimum value health insurance to a specified percentage[4] of their full-time employees and their dependents or face penalties.

---

[4] 70% in 2015 and 95% in 2016 and beyond

As simple as it sounds, this sentence is a bit more complicated than it seems. Each of these underlined words has a specific meaning under the law and it may not be a meaning you expect.

First we will explore what it means to be a "Large Employer."

Am I A Large Employer?

A Large Employer is defined as an Employer with 50 or more *Full-Time* and *Full-Time Equivalent (FTE)* Employees. Here is how you figure it out:

A	**Total number of Full-Time Employees** • A Full Time Employee is one who averages 30+ hours of service per week or 130 hours per month • ***Hours of Service*** includes all hours for which the employee is paid, including vacation, illness, disability, etc.
B	**Total number of Full-Time Equivalent Employees** Add total number of Part-Time ***Hours of Service*** in a given month and divide that number by 120.
	Add A and B together • If this number is equal to or greater than 50[5], then you are a Large Employer and must offer coverage to your Full-Time Employees or face a penalty. • Must also do "Controlled Group" Analysis to determine if your Controlled Group makes you a Large Employer.

[5] Transition Rule: Employers with less than 100 employees do not have to comply in 2015.

<u>Example</u>:

Bite-Me Burgers employs 200 Employees of which 25 are Full-Time and 175 are Part-Time.

- The total average number of Part-Time service hours paid per month to the Part-Time Employees is 13,800. 13,800 divided by 120 = 115. Bite-Me therefore has 115 Full-Time Equivalent (FTE) Employees.
- 115 (FTEs) + 25 (Full-Time Employees) = 140. 140 is more than 50 so Bite-Me is a Large Employer and is subject to the Employer Mandate.
- Under the Employer Mandate, Bite-Me must offer insurance to its 25 Full-Time Employees.

<u>Another Example</u>:

Mystery-Meat Tacos employs 65 Employees of which 25 are Full-Time and 40 are Part time.

- The total average number of Part-Time service hours paid per month to the Part-Time Employees is 2,400 divided by 120 = 20. Mystery-Meat therefore has 20 Full-Time Equivalent (FTE) Employees.
- 20 (FTEs) + 25 = 45. 45 is less than 50 so Mystery-Meat is NOT a Large Employer and is NOT subject to the Employer Mandate.

Transition Rule

Employers with less than 100 employees are exempt from penalties for the 2015 plan year.

Controlled Group Analysis

In determining if you are a Large Employer, you must also consider any partnerships or related businesses with common ownership. All of those groups together are considered a "Controlled Group." If your Controlled Group has 50+ Full-Time and Full-Time Equivalent Employees, then your Controlled Group is a Large Employer even if your entity alone would not otherwise be a Large Employer.

A Controlled Group is a group of businesses that are treated as one business for purposes of the Employer Mandate. The definition of Controlled Group includes four types:

1. **Parent-Subsidiary** – Exists when one company owns 80% or more of a subsidiary.

2. **Brother-Sister** – Five or Fewer individuals own 80% or more of two or more companies.

3. **Affiliated Services Group** – Generally applies to one or more service organizations without formal ownership ties but with close ties in providing professional services.

4. **Management Group** – This is the organization that provides management services and the organization for which the management services are provided.

****Warning:** This is a very simplified explanation of these concepts and is not a substitute for legal advice. There are many nuances to each of these concepts and you need to consult with an attorney or CPA to make sure you are protected.******

Here Are The Four Categories Explained In More Detail:

1. Parent-Subsidiary

A chain or chain of companies where a company owns 80% of the voting power or 80% of the value of the next company in the chain.

<u>**Example:**</u>

Company A owns 80% of Company B.
Company A also owns 90% of Company C.
Company C owns 65% of Company D.

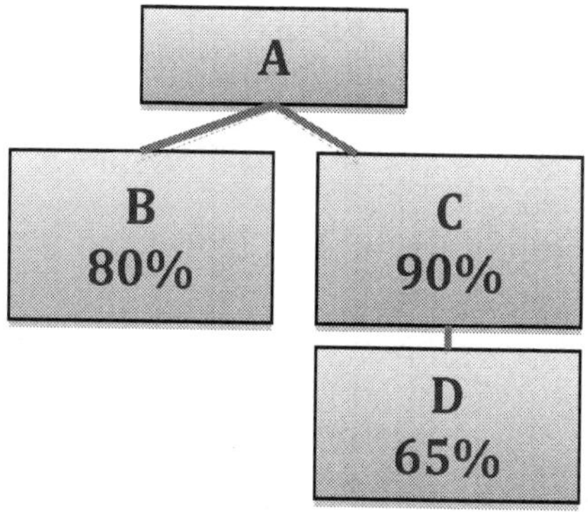

Company A, B, and C (but not D) are part of the same Parent-Subsidiary Controlled Group. This means the employees of A, B, and C all have to be counted together and if all 3 together have 50+ full-time employees and full-time equivalents, then A, B, and C are a controlled group.

Warning** This is just the beginning of the analysis. You also need to take into account **Attribution Rules** and **Exclusions.** Also, for purposes of this test, ownership includes voting power and ownership of equity value.

2. Brother-Sister

There are 3 Elements that must be met:

(a) Two or more companies
(b) The same 5 or fewer individuals together own 80% of each company; and
(c) Only taking into account such individual's *lowest percentage of ownership* of each company, the same 5 or fewer individuals own 50% of each company.

This is just the beginning of the analysis. You also need to take into account **Attribution Rules and **Exclusions.** Also, for purposes of this test, ownership includes voting power and ownership of equity value.

Example:

	Arnie	Biff	Clyde	Zeke
Company A	10%	30%	5%	55%
Company B	30%	10%	0%	60%
Company C	0%	60%	10%	30%
Company Z	5%	55%	30%	10%

- There are 4 companies and four individuals together own 100% of Companies A, B, C, and Z. This 100% is over the 80% threshold to be deemed a Brother-Sister controlled group.

- Next you take each person's lowest percentage of ownership:
  - Arnie's lowest percentage is 0% of Company C
  - Biff's lowest percentage is 10% of Company B
  - Clyde's lowest percentage is 0% of Company B
  - Zeke's lowest percentage is 10% of Company Z

- When combined, Arnie's, Biff's, Clyde's and Zeke's lowest percentage ownership in all 4 companies is 20%. 20% is lower than the 50% threshold. Therefore, this is **NOT** a Brother-Sister Controlled Group.

This illustration is meant to give you a sample of a Brother-Sister Controlled Group Analysis. There are many other pieces that go into this analysis and we strongly advise you to seek the advice of an attorney who is familiar with the ACA. For example, when you are analyzing possible brother-sister relationships, you must look at each possible pairing of businesses. In other words, even if all 4 companies don't qualify as a controlled group, 2 or 3 of the 4 might. It is really important to look at all the possibilities.

Attribution Rules. The Attribution Rules treat you as owning the interests belonging to certain people related to you (i.e. spouse, child under the age of 21, grandchildren under the age of 21, in some cases partners, trusts and estates, corporations, etc.)

3. Affiliated Services Group

This is a combination of one or more service organizations without formal ownership ties to each other, but that are closely linked to providing professional services. This group involves service providers like plumbers, electricians, law offices, health care providers, accountants, architects, insurance providers, consultants, etc.

4. Management Services Group

This is a company that principally provides management services and the organization for which services are provided.

If the Management company provides services for two or more organizations, there is no Management Services Group.

Why Is This A Planning Opportunity?

While the Controlled Group is used to determine if you are a Large Employer, the penalties are applied on an entity by entity basis.

Example:

- Companies A, B, and C are a Controlled Group.
    - Company A offers affordable, minimum value insurance to its full time employees.
    - Company B does not offer insurance to its full time employees and incurs a penalty.
    - Company C offers insurance but it is not affordable and Company C incurs a penalty.

- This is how the penalties are applied to the controlled group:
    - Company A complied with the law – no penalty.
    - Company B did not comply with the law and owes the penalty but gets a reduction of its pro rata share of the 30 employee exclusion (explained below).
    - Company C did not comply with the law and owes a penalty but does not get any reduction because this type of penalty does not allow for an exclusion.

The reason I say that this is a planning opportunity is because once you accurately understand how the penalties would be applied within each separate entity, you can start strategizing. For example, if you know the pro rata share of the 30 employee exclusion, you may determine that it makes sense not to offer insurance in one business but to offer it in another. I strongly advise consulting with either one of our advisors or your own expert to walk through this analysis so that you can make an informed decision.

Seasonal Workers

A *Seasonal Worker* is an employee who works only on a seasonal basis. The IRS regulations define a seasonal worker as an employee in a position for which the customary annual employment is six months or less. As such, if the services performed are, by their nature, not continuous throughout the year, those services may be considered seasonal.

There is a lot of confusion around the seasonal worker rules especially among my farm labor clients. I am going to clarify some things here. First of all, the typical way we think of the term "seasonal worker," is not the same way the ACA uses the term. Seasonal workers are not given any special treatment under the ACA. In fact, they are treated the in the same manner as a variable hour employee.

The only special treatment an employer gets for hiring seasonal workers is with regard to how an employer determines if they are large or small. This is referred to as the "Seasonal Worker Exception" and is defined below. Other than that, there are no other special seasonal worker rules that apply for employers.

Special Rule for Seasonal workers

- This Rule can only be used if you are an Employer who uses a 12 calendar month year counting period to determine if you are a Large Employer.

- The Rule goes like this:

  If the sum of your full-time employees and full-time equivalents exceeds 50 for 4 months (or 120 days) or less during the preceding calendar year, and the number would be less than 50 for those months if seasonal workers were excluded, you will not be considered a Large Employer in the next calendar year. The 4 months (or 120 days) need not be consecutive.

- Um… Huh?

  It is not as confusing as it seems. Here is an Example:

  Santa has a regular staff of 49 employees. He uses a 12-month counting period. Every year, Santa hires an extra 55 employees from October through December to deal with increased manufacturing demands during those months. Each of the 55 seasonal workers works 40 hours per week. If Santa had to count the hours of the seasonal help, he would be considered a Large Employer and would have to offer health insurance to his Full-Time Employees. However, because Santa's total number of FTE's + Full-Time Employees only exceeds 50 for less than 120 days, Santa can use the Seasonal worker exception and exclude the 55 seasonal workers.

What If I Am A Small Employer?

If you are a Small Employer, the Employer Mandate does not apply to you and you are not required to offer Health Coverage to your employees. However, if you do offer coverage, you will be required to offer minimum essential coverage, have a plan document and provide disclosures to your employees about the coverage you are offering. Here are the other requirements that apply to Small Employers:

- Must still provide employees with notice of the exchange.
- If offering health insurance, must report the aggregate costs on employee's W-2.
- Must withhold and report an additional 0.9% on employee compensation that exceeds $200,000.

I Am A Large Employer… Now What?

If you are a Large Employer then you are required to offer affordable and minimum value health insurance to your Full-Time Employees or pay excise taxes (many refer to these as penalties).

- You are only required to ***offer*** the coverage. If employees decline coverage, that will not trigger a penalty. ***Be sure you keep good records to prove it. A model form is attached in APPENDIX A.**

- You are only required to offer coverage to your ***Full-Time Employees*** and their dependents. There is no requirement that you offer coverage to Part-Time Employees.

Who Must Be Offered Health Coverage?

Large Employers must offer coverage to 95%[6] of their ***Full-Time Employees*** and their dependents beginning January 1, 2015. A Full-Time Employee is defined as an employee who averages **30** hours of service per week or **130** hours of service per month.

- ***Hours of Service*** are not necessarily the same as 'hours worked.' Hours of Service include any time for which an employee is paid or entitled to payment and includes sick time, vacation time, disability, etc.

- ***Dependents*** means your Full-Time Employees' children and adopted children up to age 26, but does not include spouses, step-children, foster

[6] Transition Rule: 70% in 2015.

children or any child who is a resident of another country.

- Dependents have to be offered coverage beginning in 2015.
- There is no requirement that the coverage offered to Dependents be *affordable*.
- If you do offer coverage to spouses, there is no requirement that the coverage offered be *affordable*.

Determining Who Is Full-Time

Option I: The Look-Back Method

This is one of the things I keep harping on when I say you need to be planning NOW! The Law requires you to establish who is full-time and part-time on a monthly basis. The rules have allowed employers to use an optional *Look-Back Method* in order to plan. The purpose of the Look-Back Method is to give some predictability to employers, employees and insurers. As onerous as this law is already, it would be downright impossible for employers to comply if employees could bounce between full-time and part-time status every month.

Generally speaking, the Look-Back period is a 'measuring period' and it determines your employees' status during a so-called Stability Period. If an employee is full-time during the measuring period, he or she is full-time during the Stability Period no matter how many hours he or she actually works during the Stability Period. The same is true if the employee is part-time during the measuring period. For new employees, this period is referred to as an 'initial measurement period' and for an existing employee, it is referred to as a 'standard measurement period.'

Example:

2013											
Jan	Feb	Mar	April	May	June	July	Aug	Sep	Oct	Nov	Dec
Look-back Period											

2014											
Jan	Feb	Mar	April	May	June	July	Aug	Sep	Oct	Nov	Dec
Stability Period											

If Elmer Employee is Full-time during the Look-back Period, he is Full-Time during the Stability Period, *no matter how many hours he actually works.*

The planning comes in because you might choose a long measuring period if you employ a lot of seasonal and variable hour employees. Conversely, you might opt for a shorter measuring period if you want more flexibility to reorganize your work force.

The other reason planning is required here is because you will probably want to incorporate an "Administrative Period." You are permitted to have up to a 90-day Administrative Period each year. If you used the full 90-day Administrative Period in a given year, it would look like this:

2013											
Jan	Feb	Mar	April	May	June	July	Aug	Sep	Oct	Nov	Dec
									Look-back Period		

2014											
Jan	Feb	Mar	April	May	June	July	Aug	Sep	Oct	Nov	Dec
Look-back Period Con't.									Admin. Period		

2015											
Jan	Feb	Mar	April	May	June	July	Aug	Sep	Oct	Nov	Dec
Stability Period											

- **Why is this Significant?**

If you have employees that bounce above and below 30 hours per week, the Look-Back Method provides you with a tool to prove to the IRS their exact status over time. Records are going to be king next year when the IRS comes a knocking. If you were paying your employees for over 30 hours per week and you do not offer them insurance when the Employer Mandate kicks in, you could face big penalties.

The other reason this is significant, is that you need to plan ahead of time. You can't go back and undo something you did during your look-back period. Even if you were scheduling more employees full-time than you would have if you had planned, you are stuck with those numbers for the entire stability period.

- **Just Give Me the Basics:**

There are 3 things you need to understand about the Look-Back Method:

1. **Standard Measurement Period**
   - This is where you track your employee's hours for purposes of determining their status.
   - For ongoing employees, it must be between 3 and 12 months.
   - This can coincide with your payroll periods.

2. **Administrative Period**
   - This is an optional period of up to 90 days during which time employers can offer coverage and enroll their eligible employees. It takes place at the end of the measurement period and before the stability period.

3. **Stability Period**
   - If an employee was full-time during the Standard Measurement Period, he must be treated as full-time during the Stability Period as long as that employee remains employed and *regardless of his actual hours during the Stability Period.*

⇒ If an employee is deemed *full-time* during the Standard Measurement Period, the Stability Period must be at least 6 consecutive months and no shorter than the Standard Measurement Period.

⇒ Example: If the Standard Measurement Period is 6 months, the Stability Period is 6 months. If the Standard Measurement Period is 3 months, the Stability Period is still 6 months because that is the minimum.

- If an employee was part-time during the Standard Measurement Period, he *may* be treated as part-time during the Stability Period.

⇒ If an employee is deemed *part-time* during the Standard Measurement Period, the Stability Period must be no longer than the Standard Measurement Period.

⇒ Example: If the Standard Measurement Period is 3 months, the Measurement Period is 3 months. There is no minimum if the employee is deemed part-time.

⇒ Currently the regulations state that if an employee was part-time during the look-back period, the employer "can" treat that employee as part-time during the stability period. This is pretty wishy-washy language. The safe bet is to assume that if someone is part-time during the look-back period, but is consistently employed full-time during the stability period, that person should be offered insurance within 90* days of becoming consistently full-time. (*60 days in California.)

- If you utilize a "gap" month between the stability period and the next stability period, you must treat employees the same as they were treated prior to the "gap" month.

In general, the Standard measurement period and stability period must be the same for all employees in the same category (i.e. salaried employees, hourly employees, collectively bargained employees, each group of collectively bargained employees, employees in different states, etc.).

Transition Rule

For 2015 only, a Large Employer may use a shorter Look-Back period (e.g. 6 months) with a longer Stability Period (e.g. 12 months).

Additional Look-Back Method Rules:

1. **Reasonable Expectations.**
   An employee's status as full-time or variable hour depends on whether or not you *reasonably expect* that employee to work an average of 30 service hours per week. Here are some factors that suggest "*reasonable expectations*:
   - Is the employee replacing a full-time employee?
   - Are other employees in the same or comparable positions full-time?

- Was the job advertised as a full-time job?

2. **What if I hire a new full-time (not seasonal) employee in the middle of my measurement or stability period?**

   If you 'reasonably expect' your new employee to work full-time (an average of 30 service hours per week), you must offer them health insurance within 90 days (60 days in California unless you are self-insuring) of hire.

3. **What if I hire a new variable hour (not seasonal) employee in the middle of my measurement or stability period?**

   If it cannot be determined whether a new employee will reasonably be expected to work an average of 30 service hours per week, then you may use an 'initial measurement period' of 3 to 12 months to determine that employee's status. The stability period for such an employee, however, must be the same as the stability period for other employees in the same category. If the employee is deemed full-time during the initial measurement period, she must be considered full-time during the stability period (which can be no less than 6 months). If the employee is deemed part-time during the initial measurement period, she may be considered part-time during the stability period unless you change her status to full-time.

4. **What if I terminate and rehire the same employee?**

   The IRS is not going to let employers skirt these requirements by simply terminating an employee and rehiring her in order to start the waiting period clock ticking again. To prevent this practice, the code adopted a special rule in this instance.

   ⇒ The basic rule of thumb is that if such an employee has no hours of service for a minimum of **13 consecutive weeks,** then you can treat that employee as a new hire upon their return.

   ⇒ The alternate rule is that an employee returning from unpaid leave can be treated as a new hire if the employee had no service hours for between 4 and 13 weeks and that period is longer than the employee's period of employment before the absence.
   Example: If you have an employee that works for you for 6 weeks, leaves for 7 weeks and then you rehire him, you can treat that employee as a new employee with a new waiting period.

5. **What if an employee returns after taking an unpaid leave?**

   ⇒ This rule applies to employees who take leave pursuant to the Family and Medical Leave Act and the Uniformed Services Employment and Reemployment Rights Act and after an unpaid leave on account of jury duty.

⇒ The employer must figure out the employee's average hours of service during the measurement period excluding the weeks during which the employee was on leave. This average becomes that employee's average for the measurement period.

6. Seasonal workers

"Seasonal worker" means an employee in a position for which the customary annual employment is 6 months or less. Typically, the period of employment should begin at the same time of the year each year (e.g. summer or winter). An employee can still be considered seasonal if the season is extended.

The fact that the regulations defined seasonal workers can be a bit confusing because seasonal workers are treated the same as variable hour employees. This means, if your seasonal workers satisfy the conditions set forth in the Look-Back Method and they have not been separated from employment for the requisite time period to consider them a new hire, you have to offer them insurance.

Farm Labor: It is not clear in the regulations or the official commentary whether or not a break in service due to the end of a growing season, will qualify as a break in service triggering the 13-week rule. Such a reading would directly contradict the purpose of the look-back method, which is to ensure that an employee who worked full-time during a particular measurement period receives insurance during the matching stability period. Unfortunately, there will be uncertainty on this point until official guidance is given or until a brave employer wants to take on the risk associated being wrong. If wrong, an employer could face a $2,000 per employee per month penalty for not offering insurance after instituting the 13-week rule. Until definitive guidance is given or if you are that brave employer ready to take on the IRS, it is recommended that you continue to offer insurance during the entire stability period, even if the growing season has ended. There are low cost, minimum essential coverage insurance plans that are designed specifically for you.

7. **Change in Status**

If your employee's status changes from part-time to full-time during the initial measurement period, you must offer that employee insurance by the earlier of 1st day of the 4th month following the change in employment or the 1st day of the 4th month following the end of the initial measurement period plus any administrative period.

Option II: The Monthly Measurement Period

If you choose not to use the Look-Back/Stability Method, you will most likely use the Monthly Measurement method to identify your full-time employees. This is a method whereby employers count the hours of service for each calendar month. Here are the rules that apply if you use this method:

1. **Eligible Employee's First Date of Eligibility**
   An eligible employee must be offered coverage by the 1st day of the 4th calendar month after such employee becomes "otherwise eligible" for an offer of coverage. "Otherwise eligible" means the employee has met all conditions required to become eligible other than the completion of a waiting period.

2. **Weekly Rule**
   This rule is designed to coincide with payroll periods. If you choose to use this method, you can determine full-time status for a calendar month based on service hours over successive 4-week and 5-week periods.
   - The period measured for the month must include *either* the week that contains the first day of the month or the week that contains the last, but not both.
   - For calendar months using 4-week periods, 120 hours of service is full-time.
   - For calendar months using 5-week periods, 150 hours of service is full-time.

3. **130 Hour Equivalency**
   An employer may treat 130 service hours per month as equivalent to 30 hours per week.

4. **Break in Service/Rehire Rules**
   The same rules apply using the Monthly Measurement method as described above in the Look-Back Method.
   - The basic rule of thumb is that if such an employee has no hours of service for a minimum of **13 consecutive weeks,** then you can treat that employee as a new hire upon their return.
   - The alternate rule is that an employee returning from unpaid leave can be treated as a new hire if the employee had no service hours for between 4 and 13 weeks and that period is longer than the employee's period of employment before the absence.

<u>Example</u>: If you have an employee that works for you for 6 weeks, leaves for 7 weeks and then you rehire him, you can treat that employee as a new employee with a new waiting period.

Measurement Methods	
Look-Back Method	• Typically used for hourly employees • Reasonable Expectation of New Employee's Status - Replacing full-time employee - Comparable positions - How job was advertised • Full Time - Minimum measurement period is 3 months with minimum 6 month stability period • Part Time – Measurement period matches the stability period • Seasonal Employee treated as variable • Change in employment status. • Transition Rule – for 2015, employers can use a 6-month measurement period beginning in July with a corresponding 12 month stability period.
Monthly Measurement Method	• Employer counts employees' hours during a particular month to see if employee was full-time (at least 30 ser vice hours) for that month. • Weekly Rule can be used to accommodate payroll periods - The period measured for the month must include either the week that contains the first day of the month or the week that contains the last, but not both. - For calendar months using 4-week periods, 120 hours of service is full-time. - For calendar months using 5-week periods, 150 hours of service is full-time. • Employer may treat 130 service hours per month as equivalent to 30 hours per week

Ninety-Day Waiting Period

You can impose up to a 90-day waiting period before you offer insurance to all new employees and to all newly eligible employees. California has reduced this number to 60 for plans falling under its jurisdiction. Note that self-insured plans are governed by ERISA which is federal law and is exempt from California's 60 day rule.

The 90-day waiting period is significant in certain industries with high turnover and in industries that employ variable hour and seasonal workers. Often employees in these situations will not stay long enough to qualify for coverage.

A violation of this provision can result in penalties of $100 per employee per day up to statutory minimums. The rules related to the waiting period are complex. The gist of it is that the waiting period is the maximum time that can pass before coverage for an individual who is otherwise eligible to enroll under the terms of a group health plan can become effective.

Limited Non-Assessment Period For Certain Employees

No assessment (penalty) is owed in the following circumstances:

- The first 3 months after an employee first becomes otherwise eligible for coverage under the monthly measurement method.

- The months of January through March of the first year that the employer becomes an applicable large employer so long as any employee who was not offered coverage by the employer during the previous calendar year is offered coverage by April 1st of the year the employer became an applicable large employer.

- A new full-time employee as long as they are offered coverage on the first day of the month following the first 3 calendar months of employment.

- During the initial measurement and administrative periods for variable, seasonal and part-time employees.

- If an employee is in his initial measurement period and there is a change to full-time status as long as coverage is offered on the 1st day of the 4th month after such change.

- The month that an employee is hired, if he is hired on a day that is not the first day of the month.

- The month that a full-time employee terminates.

Just tell me what I need to do please…

I promised to be straight with you and tell you what I think you need to really understand and when you should seek guidance. This is one of those areas where there is a ton of information and guidance available. For companies that have a large number of variable hour and seasonal workers, keeping track of their hours and critical dates for compliance issues could be a nightmare. There is software out there and companies providing services to help employer track this information. When you consider that the documents you keep will be the only way you will be able to challenge a penalty assessment, using a service like this is not a bad idea. If you do not use a service like this, you better make sure that your documents are thorough and up to date. Make sure that you are keeping track of the dates that you have to offer coverage as well as proof that you did in fact offer coverage and to whom.

There are advantages and disadvantages to choosing different measurement periods (although I have never advised anyone to use anything other than a 12 month measurement period). The analysis is going to be specific to your organization.

When you hear about companies 'scheduling down to part-time,' this is why they are doing it. They want to show that their employees were part-time during the initial measurement period. In my practice, I have seen that this is sometimes easier said than done. While many business owners intend to schedule down to part-time, they are learning too late that a number of their employees in fact worked over 30 hours. For those that began planning soon enough, they will be able to adjust those employees' hours for the remainder of the measurement period. For those employers who have not even begun, this is just one of the challenges ahead. The latest IRS regulations said that after February 9, 2014, a reduction in workforce size or overall hours of service to avoid the employer mandate will be considered not to have happened.

The other challenge posed by this strategy is that employers who do "schedule down to part-time" are going to need to clearly establish that they did it for a business reason and did not do it to avoid offering benefits. There are ERISA litigators waiting to file lawsuits against employers who cut employees' hours to avoid paying them insurance benefits and unless the employer can prove otherwise, those lawyers are going to win. Not only that, employers are now on notice that the IRS will not consider such a reduction to have happened if it was not due to a clear business reason (e.g. sale of a division, layoffs due to poor performance, or changes in the economic marketplace in which the employer operates).

Before cutting employees hours to part-time there are many things that you need to consider:

1. Can you establish that you have a legitimate business purpose for cutting hours? Is this policy reflected in your hiring practices and policies, in your employee handbooks and job descriptions?

2. How will this impact your customer service and employee morale?

3. How are you communicating this? More importantly, how are your managers communicating this? One text from a manager telling an employee that his hours are being cut because of Obamacare is going to be Exhibit A in a courtroom for many unlucky employers (I have actually seen these texts – don't think it can't happen to you).

4. Have you examined all of your other options? Cutting hours may not be the best option for everyone. For example, there are self-insurance programs out there that allow you to fund your Obamacare compliance using money you save in insurance premiums. This mechanism completely bypasses the need to cut employees' hours, which is important for employers who can't properly run their business with a part-time workforce or who can't prove that cutting hours is for any reason other than to avoid the mandates.

ACTION STEPS

1. Figure out if you are a Large Employer or a Small Employer.

2. If you own more than one company or have partners, find out if you are a Controlled Group. If you own many stores or businesses under one legal entity, consult with a lawyer about doing some planning to take advantage of the Controlled Group rules limiting penalties to each individual entity within the Controlled Group.

3. If you employ seasonal workers, be sure you are aware of the Seasonal worker Rules. You will probably want to use a 12-month counting period to determine if you are a Large Employer.

4. If you are a Small Employer, make sure you are providing the required disclosures to your employees.

5. If you are a Large Employer, determine if you are going to use a Monthly Measurement Period or a Look-Back Method.

6. Establish procedures and a documentation process to track your Look-Back Method.

7. If you are considering employing part-time employees and reducing the number of full-time employees you employ, get the advice of an employment attorney. Be sure your employee handbooks, policies and procedures are coordinated to establish the business purposes behind taking such an approach.

8. Institute a 90-Day Administrative Period.

Chapter 3:
I is for Insurance

Everybody has a plan until they get punched in the face.
~Mike Tyson

If you are in fact a Large Employer, it is not enough to offer just any old insurance. The law is very specific about what kind of insurance you have to offer. In this Chapter, I am going to give you the cheat sheet to understanding these requirements and some tips to help you avoid funding the law through paying penalties. I am also going to give you the low down on the Insurance Marketplace (also called the Insurance Exchange) and the subsidies. Last but not least, I will explain how your decisions will directly impact your employees' eligibility for the subsidies and why you should care.

What Is The Insurance Marketplace?

The Insurance Marketplace or Insurance Exchange is where individuals and small businesses can go to purchase insurance from participating private health insurance companies. One of the common misconceptions is that the exchanges are going to be selling government run health insurance or that there is only one type of policy available on the exchanges.

The truth is that the ACA put in place new requirements governing "how" insurance policies could be sold and what insurance policies had to cover. Private insurance companies that choose to comply with these rules compete with each other on the exchanges.

Under the law, all states were originally required to create their own websites (similar to a Travelocity® or Expedia®) where an individual could enter their information and learn about all the programs for which he or she is eligible. Implementation was delayed from the original date, and the rollout of the federal exchange was a bit of a disaster. Unfortunately, the result has been a disjointed federal system that has been unpredictable at best. Some states have created their own exchanges and residents of the states that did not will be expected to utilize the federal exchange.

The idea is that individuals will be able to purchase Minimum Essential Coverage health insurance on the exchange from private insurance companies. The Small Business Health Options Program (SHOP) Exchange will be available to certain small businesses. The website to access the Exchanges is: http://www.Healthcare.gov

Premium and Cost-Sharing Subsidies: Beginning in 2014, financial assistance will be available to individuals and families earning up to 400% of the federal poverty line. For example, this means that an individual earning up to $45,960 or a family of 4 earning up to $94,200 will be eligible for some sort of subsidy. Here is the breakdown of the Federal Poverty guidelines that will be used to calculate premiums and subsidies in new guidelines that are adopted:

Household Size	100%	133%	138%	150%	200%	300%	400%
1	$11,490	$15,282	$15,856	$17,235	$22,980	$34,470	$45,960
2	$15,510	$20,628	$21,404	$23,265	$31,020	$46,530	$62,040
3	$19,530	$25,975	$26,951	$29,295	$39,060	$58,590	$78,120
4	$23,550	$31,322	$32,499	$35,325	$47,100	$70,650	$94,200
5	$27,570	$36,668	$38,047	$41,355	$55,140	$82,710	$110,280
6	$31,590	$42,015	$43,594	$47,385	$63,180	$94,770	$126,360
7	$35,610	$47,361	$49,142	$53,415	$71,220	$106,830	$142,440
8	$39,630	$52,708	$54,689	$59,445	$79,260	$118,890	$158,520
For each additional person, add	$4,020	$5,347	$5,548	$6,030	$8,040	$12,060	$16,080

The amount of assistance available will depend on income and the type of insurance plan selected (i.e. bronze, silver, gold, platinum).

- Premium Assistance Tax Credits will be available to help lower the premium amount individuals and families must pay for their coverage.

- Cost Sharing Assistance will be available to help limit the individual's maximum out of pocket costs and reduce the cost sharing amounts (i.e. deductibles and co-pays) that would otherwise be charged.

Eligibility for Subsidies: Any individual who is eligible for an employer-sponsored plan is not eligible to receive financial assistance or a subsidy on the insurance exchanges.

- This means that a child who is eligible to receive health insurance from his parent's employer, cannot qualify for a subsidy on the exchange. This is very significant because the employer is not required to make insurance offered to an employee's dependent "affordable." In other words, the employer can require the dependent to pay for 100% of the cost of the premium, and even if the dependent declines the coverage because the coverage was too expensive, the dependent will be unable to receive a subsidy.
- Unlike dependents, employers are not required to offer insurance to the spouses of employees. However, if the employer does offer the coverage, there is no requirement that the insurance offered be "affordable." Furthermore, if the employer does offer spousal coverage, the spouse becomes ineligible to receive a subsidy on the exchange, even if the spouse declines the coverage.

It is very important to understand this concept so you know the implications of your plan on your employees and their families.

Open Enrollment: Despite what many people believe, individuals cannot purchase insurance on the exchange at any time they wish. The exchanges use an open enrollment period that coincides with the Medicare open enrollment period. Without an enrollment period, people might not enroll until they get sick, which ends up costing insurance companies more money.

What Type Of Coverage Must I Offer?

If you are a Large Employer, you must offer your Full-Time Employees and their Dependents* **Minimum Essential Coverage** that is **Affordable** and **Minimum Value**.

*Currently, employers must offer dependent coverage beginning in 2015.

➢ **What Is Minimum Essential Coverage (MEC)?**

- Generally, MEC is any coverage that satisfies the ACA mandates. For traditional small group insurance plans, this includes the so-called Essential Health Benefits. Large Group and Self-Insured plans are exempt from some, but not all, of these requirements.

- **MEC Provisions:**
  1. No one can be denied for a pre-existing condition (often referred to as "guaranteed issue")
  2. No Annual Limits of Lifetime Limits for Essential Health Benefits

  3. Must cover Essential Health Benefits which are broadly defined as:
     - Ambulatory patient services;
     - Emergency services;
     - Hospitalization;
     - Maternity and newborn care;
     - Mental health and substance use disorder services, including behavioral health treatment;
     - Prescription drugs;
     - Rehabilitative and habilitative services and devices;
     - Laboratory services;
     - Preventive and wellness services and chronic disease management; and
     - Pediatric services, including oral and vision care

  4. Maximum Out of Pocket Costs (the amount you can require your plan participants to pay for co-pays and deductibles)
     - For traditional insured plan, it is generally $6,350 for an individual plan and $12,700 for a family plan.

- Self-insured plans have more flexibility with these rules and may in some instances require higher out of pockets from plan participants.

5. Preventative and wellness services at no cost sharing to the insured.

6. Excise Tax on High-Cost Coverage (Cadillac Tax)
   - Beginning in 2018, a 40 percent excise tax will be imposed on the value of health insurance benefits exceeding a certain threshold.
   - The thresholds are $10,200 for individual coverage and $27,500 for family coverage (indexed to inflation).
   - The thresholds increase for individuals in high-risk professions and for employers that have a disproportionately older population.
   - Employers who exceed the Excise Tax Limits by even a small amount can end up paying significant, non-deductible penalties.

➤ What Is Affordable Coverage?

Coverage is **Affordable** if your employee's share of the premium for insurance for himself does not exceed 9.5% of his household income.

How the heck are you going to be able to figure out your employee's household income? Funny you should ask… the IRS has provided three optional safe harbors for determining household income. An employer may use the same safe harbor for all of its employees or it may use different safe harbors for different reasonable categories of employees.

The reasonable categories include (1) manner of compensation (e.g. salary vs. hourly); (2) specified job categories; (3) geographic location; and (4) similar bona fide business criteria.

Summary of the 3 Safe Harbors:

1. **Federal Poverty Line**
   - Each employee's contribution for self-only coverage cannot exceed 9.5% of the most recently published federal poverty line for a single individual.
   - This safe harbor allows for simplicity in that you charge the same premium contribution even if the employee's wages fluctuate slightly.
   - If the current federal poverty guidelines have not yet been released at the time of the employer's open enrollment, the employer can use the federal poverty guidelines in effect six months prior to the beginning of the plan year.

2. **Rate of Pay**
   - Each employee's contribution for self-only coverage cannot exceed 9.5% of his monthly pay.
   - Use monthly salary for salaried employees.
   - For hourly employees multiply the hourly rate by 130 hours.

- This safe harbor may be used even if you reduce the employee's hourly wage during the year.
- This safe harbor may be used for salaried employees, but only if the monthly salary is not reduced.

3. W-2

- Each employee's contribution for self-only coverage cannot exceed 9.5% of the amount reported in Box 1 of his W-2 for the calendar year.
- When you use this method, you may only look at the current calendar year W-2 wages (as opposed to the wages from the previous year).
- Employers may not add any salary reduction elections (e.g. 401(k) or cafeteria plan) back into the W-2 to determine affordability.

➢ What Is Minimum Value Coverage?

Minimum value means that the health plan is designed to pay at least 60% of the total cost of medical services for a standard population. This is an actuarial calculation. Actuarial calculations are quite complex and this is a very simplified explanation of what it entails.

One of the things that changed under the ACA is that in order to be Minimum Value, health insurance plans must cover things like preventative and wellness and a variety of mandated coverages. In order to come up with the 60% actuarial value, the insurance company looks at the different things that must be covered. For some things, the insurance company is allowed to collect co-pays and deductible from the beneficiary.

Insurance companies are now required to cover 100% of the cost of preventative and wellness and are not permitted to require any cost sharing from beneficiaries for those services. After that, the insurance company may require the insured to pay co-pays and deductibles but only so long as the policy ends up paying at least 60% of the total cost of the medical services covered. A plan at the 60% actuarial value is considered a "Bronze Plan."

The different so-called 'metal' plans have different actuarial values:

- Bronze (60%)
- Silver (70%)
- Gold (80%)
- Platinum (90%)

What Does It Mean To 'Offer' Coverage?

The ACA requires applicable large employers "offer" insurance coverage to their full-time employers. The law does not specify what an employer must do to demonstrate that it made an offer of coverage. However, if one of your full-time employees declines your offer of coverage, gets a subsidy on the exchange and later claims you never offered coverage, you are could be assessed a penalty. Therefore, it is very important that you document every offer of coverage including the amount of time your employees were given to accept or decline coverage. I also recommend that you require each employee to decline coverage in writing and that you retain such documents in case you are audited.

The Regulations have also clarified some additional rules regarding what constitutes an "offer" under the ACA:

- **Third Party Offer of Coverage**
  If an employee receives on offer from a third party employer (e.g. a PEO or staffing firm) on behalf of the client employer, that offer qualifies as an offer by the client employer as long as the client employer pays a higher fee for such employee than it would otherwise pay.

- **Multiple Employer and Single Employer Taft-Hartley Plans and MEWAs**
  If the employer contributed to the plan on behalf of the employee, this constitutes as an offer of coverage.

- **Collective Bargaining**
  In a collective bargaining scenario between a union and an employer, where the union rejects the coverage, this is not considered an offer of coverage to the employers.

- **Multiple Employers**
  If an employee is employed by more than one applicable large employer for a given month, an offer of coverage by one applicable large

employer qualifies as an offer of coverage for all applicable large employers for that month.

- **Employees Who Have Other Insurance Coverage**
  The fact that a full-time employee has other insurance coverage (either through a spouse, Medicare, Medicaid, etc.) does not negate the employer's responsibility to offer that employee coverage. Such an employee cannot be the "trigger" of a penalty because someone who is receiving Medicaid or Medicare would not be eligible for a subsidy or a premium tax credit. However, such an employee will still be counted if you are subject to Penalty A.

Will Insurance Costs Increase?

This is an interesting question and the misinformation in the media has made it quite confusing. Some states are reporting that their insurance costs have increased while other states are saying their insurance costs have decreased. How can this be?

Many employers are reporting the same confusion among the quotes they are receiving from the insurance companies. There is no doubt that it will take some time before we know exactly how market conditions will impact insurance prices. There are some things we do know though.

In general, health costs have consistently increased at a rate faster than the rate of overall inflation. In addition to this steady trend, there are some very basic concepts that explain what we are seeing and will continue to see in the insurance market.

Prior to the ACA, insurance companies used to control their costs by denying people coverage if they had pre-existing conditions, only covering certain procedures and having lifetime limits on coverage. The ACA prohibits insurance companies from denying for pre-existing conditions or from having lifetime caps and requires insurance policies to include preventative and wellness coverage at no cost-sharing to the individual. As a result, the insurance company now knows it is going to have to pay out more in claims than it used to.

The other piece to this is that the ACA is making insurance available to millions of people who could not get insurance previously. It is likely that the people who need it the most and will cost the insurance companies the most money are the ones who are going to sign up first. This creates a scenario called 'adverse selection.' If this happens, then the cost of the insurance will go up even more so that the insurance company can collect enough premium to pay the claims and still make their profits.

The third piece to this puzzle relates to risk pools. When insurance companies sell insurance to a business, they typically have a mandatory participation requirement - which means that the employer has to guaranty that at least 75-80% of their employees will take the coverage. By doing this, the insurance company can set their rates based on empirical data that tells them how much they can anticipate paying out in claims based on the demographics in the risk pool. In other words, the healthy people in the group bring down the costs for the sick people.

This same principle applies in the exchanges. The insurance companies in the exchanges are private insurance companies that are competing with other private insurance companies. If the exchanges only get the sick people, then the insurance companies in the exchange cannot pay claims and still make the kind of profit they like to make. Obamacare attempts to manage this through the Individual Mandate (requiring everyone to have insurance) and encouraging young, healthy people to buy insurance through the exchange. This is also why the Administration is often quoted as saying that it is important to get the young, healthy people into the exchanges.

So, will insurance costs increase? The math says yes. However, external factors such as creative calculations, excise taxes and subsidies could make it seem like they are not.

ACA Non-Discrimination Rules

The Law states that health plans may not discriminate in favor of highly compensated employees. However, as of the date of this publication, no specific guidance has been issued on this topic for traditional insurance plans. Self-insured plans still have to comply with the ERISA non-discrimination rules. Employers offering traditional insurance are not bound by the ACA nondiscrimination rules until such guidance is issued. The commentary from the IRS has stated that once non-discrimination rules are released, employers will be given time to comply.

It is very important to stay on top of this because once released, violating the non-discrimination rules can carry a $100 per employee per day penalty.

ACTION STEPS

1. If you are purchasing traditional insurance, make sure that your insurance broker is well-versed on the ACA. If not, find one who is.

2. If you are a Large Employer, you need to be working with your insurance broker to find the best insurance product for your company.

3. If you are a Large Employer, you should educate yourself on all of your options including self-insurance.

4. Look at your workforce and determine which safe harbor you intend to use to meet the "Affordability" requirement.

5. Start getting a plan in place for how you plan to keep records. Any time an employee declines coverage, you must get it in writing. Otherwise, if that employee later gets a subsidy on the exchange, you could be subjected to penalties.

6. If you are already offering insurance, be sure you are providing the proper disclosures to your employees.

Chapter 4:
P is for Penalties

The only difference between death and taxes is that death does not get worse every time Congress meets.
~Will Rogers

A major source of funding of the ACA is through excise taxes (penalties) paid by employers and individuals. Each time an employer is subject to a penalty, the IRS will notify the employer and give them an opportunity to respond before assessing liability or demanding payment. Based on the commentary released in the federal regulations, it is expected that such employer notices will be sent out after the date that individual tax returns are due for each given year. That is expected to be a minimum of 18 months after the fact. This is especially frightening because an employer may not be aware that they were in violation until they have been in violation for nearly 2 years. This could get very costly and is even more reason why employers need to be educated on the ACA.

In this chapter, I am going to explain the details behind these penalties.

Overview Of Penalties

Employers who fail to comply with the Employer Mandate will be subject to Excise Taxes. I often refer to them as penalties because if you have to pay them, they are going to feel like penalties. There are two different types of penalties for failing to comply with the Employer Mandate:

Penalty A

If you are a Large Employer and you **do not offer** coverage to at least 95%[7] your full-time **employees.**

Penalty B

You are a Large Employer and offer coverage to your full-time employers but it is **not affordable** or **does not provide minimum value**.

Let's discuss each penalty in more detail:

PENALTY A: Employer Does Not Offer Coverage

- **How much is the Penalty?**
  $2,000 per year x total number of full-time employees.
  (even if you are providing insurance to some or even a majority *of those full-time employees)*

[7] Transition Rule: 70% in 2015.

- **Less 30[8]:**
  No Penalty is paid for the first 30 employees. However, if you are part of a controlled group, the 30 free employees are shared pro rata among each entity in the controlled group.

- **How is it triggered:**
  Taking into account the Margin of Error Rule below, as soon as one employee receives a premium tax credit or a cost-sharing subsidy on the Exchange, the penalty is triggered for *all* full-time employees, even the ones you are offering insurance. This can be very expensive, especially if you are already paying for insurance to some or a majority of your full-time employees.

- **Margin of Error Rule**
  This rule requires 95%[9] compliance. Therefore, if you do not offer coverage to only 5% of your full-time employees, you will not be penalized.

Example (not a Controlled Group): Woozy Wineries employs 100 full-time employees. Woozy is pretty sure none of his employees are going to want insurance because it is too expensive. Woozy prices out different insurance plans, decides it is too expensive and opts to take a gamble and not offer any

[8] Transition Rule: Less 80 in 2015.

[9] Transition Rule: 70% in 2015.

coverage at all. One of Woozy's employees, Gilbert Grape goes to the exchange and qualifies for a premium tax credit (note – if Woozy had offered insurance, none of his employees would have been able to qualify for a tax credit). Woozy is now on the hook to pay the IRS $140,000 ($2,000 x 100 less the first 30). There is no deduction available to Woozy on the tax, but there would have been a deduction on the cost of the premium if Woozy had decided to offer insurance.

Example (Controlled Group): Pelosi owns 50% of Pizza Parliament, which has 25 full-time employees and 50% of Burger Hut, which also has 25 full-time employees. Her business partner, Cruz, owns the other 50% of Pizza Parliament and the other 50% of Burger Hut. Pizza Parliament and Burger Hut are a Controlled Group, are subject to the Employer Mandate and therefore must offer health insurance to all full-time employees or pay a penalty.

Pizza Parliament does not offer insurance, but Burger Hut does. Pizza Parliament is assessed a penalty of $20,000 ($2,000 x (25 less 50% of 30)). Pizza Parliament's pro-rata share of the 30-employee reduction is 15. This would be the result even if Burger Hut did not offer insurance.

PENALTY B: Employer Offers Coverage But It Is Not Affordable or Does Not Provide Not Minimum Value

- **How much is the Penalty?**
  The lesser of Penalty A or $3,000 per year x total number of full-time employees *who receive a premium subsidy or* cost-*sharing reduction* on the Exchange.

- **How is it triggered?**
  Any time an employee qualifies for a premium tax credit or a cost-sharing reduction on the Exchange, the penalty is triggered for that employee only.

- **No Margin of Error Allowed and No Less 30.**

Example: Nate's Nut Growers has 100 employees and decides to offer insurance. However, Nate did not read this book and did not understand that he could not require his employees to pay more than 9.5% of their income toward the premium, so he charged them each 15% of their income. Nate's insurance was also did not provide Minimum Value because the coverage did not include the federally required preventative and wellness services at no cost sharing to his employees. Nate was surprised to find out that 50 of his employees bought insurance on the exchange and qualified for some sweet subsidies. As a result, Nate was charged a penalty of $150,000 ($3,000 x 50). Nate could not take advantage of any margin of error rules nor the less 30 rule and his penalties were not deductible.

Things To Consider

- Consider how likely it will be for your employees to qualify for a premium tax credit or a subsidy. If your business employs minimum or lower wage workers, your employees will likely qualify for the credit or the subsidy.

- If one of your employees does in fact qualify for a credit or a subsidy on the Exchange, the IRS will give you notice. The only way to avoid paying a penalty at that point is if you have documentation proving that (1) you offered Minimum Essential Coverage insurance to your employees; (2) your employee declined coverage; (3) your employee was not full-time or (4) you were not a large employer.

- Penalties are defined on an annual basis but they are assessed on a monthly basis.

- Penalties are not tax deductible but insurance premiums are.

- If your employees qualify for Medicare or Medicaid, they are not eligible to receive a subsidy or tax credit and therefore cannot trigger a penalty. Watch out for this one though. Just because you think your employees are eligible for some other insurance, you are not excused of your obligation to offer them coverage. If you later find out that they did in fact receive a subsidy on the exchange, you could be subject to a penalty.

Other Penalties To Watch Out For

In addition to the A and B penalties, there are other penalties to watch out for.

1. **$100 Per Employee Per Day.**
   The catchall penalty for failure to comply with the law is $100 per employee per day up to statutory maximums. Considering you will often not know you are subject to this penalty until you are being audited and likely have been in violation for an extended length of time, this penalty can become quite high.

2. **OSHA Whistleblower Protection**
   The Occupational Safety & Health Administration will be policing whistleblower claims under the Affordable Care Act. The ACA prohibits retaliation against employees who have received cost sharing reductions or tax subsidies on a Health Insurance Exchange. The standard of proof to establish a whistleblower protection claim is very low and should leave employers on high alert.

   Activities such as discharging or disciplining could be grounds for a whistleblower claim if the employee reasonably believes it was in retaliation for him having received a subsidy on the insurance exchange.

During my time as General Counsel of a pizza franchise, I often advised the CEO that the only lawsuit you win is the lawsuit you never enter. Even if you win these actions and prove you had grounds for the action taken, you still have to defend them, which takes time and money. The only way to win these actions is to avoid them in the first place.

Some ways to avoid this pitfall include:

(1) Offer insurance to your full-time employees (anyone offered qualified employer sponsored coverage cannot qualify for a subsidy and therefore no whistleblower protection);

(2) Train all of your managers and HR on proper documentation and protocol when disciplining or terminating any employee that works for you;

(3) Do not offer financial incentives to employees in return for not applying for financial assistance on the exchange.

3. Exchange Notification

Although there is no penalty associated with this, all Employers are required to give their employees notice of the Insurance Marketplace (Insurance Exchange). I recommend compliance because among other things, it will not look good during your audit if you tell your IRS agent that you decided to pick and choose which provisions you would like to follow.

- All initial notices were due by October 1, 2013.
- All new employees must be given this notice within 14 days of being hired.
- A model notice is attached as **APPENDIX B.**

4. **Excise Tax on High-Cost Coverage (Cadillac Tax)**

Beginning in 2018, a 40 percent excise tax will be imposed on the value of health insurance benefits exceeding a certain threshold. The thresholds are $10,200 for individual coverage and $27,500 for family coverage (indexed to inflation). The thresholds increase for individuals in high-risk professions and for employers that have a disproportionately older population.

This is not a provision to ignore. The Congressional Budget Office estimated in its May 2013 report that it will collect $80 Billion between 2013 and 2023 from the Cadillac tax. The cited purpose of this tax is to reduce overall health care costs, to address the unequal tax benefit to those who receive high value tax plans with pre-tax dollars and of course, to help finance the ACA.

Employers who exceed the Excise Tax Limits by even a small amount can end up seeing significant, non-deductible penalties.

Audits And Documentation

If you have not heard by now, the IRS has hired thousands of new IRS agents to implement the ACA. The success of the law requires the collection of billions of dollars of penalties from individuals and mostly from employers.

Here is how it will work. Every time one of your employees applies for financial assistance on the insurance exchange, you can anticipate a verification request from the insurance exchange. Employers will be required to respond to insurance exchange requests real time and on an ongoing basis.

After the date that tax returns are required to be filed, the IRS will then estimate what it believes each employer's penalties are and will send each employer a demand notice. Each employer will then have the right to rebut the IRS's estimate by providing detailed documentation. The IRS has said it may take as long as 18 months to reconcile all of the data it anticipates it will receive. That means that employers must be prepared to substantiate their claims for a period of nearly 2 years. Not only that, because this data will become part of permanent tax files, employers will be required to maintain all related documentation for a period of 7 years.

Some commentators have predicted that not only

will virtually every single applicable large employer in the United States be required to respond to a demand for documentation from the IRS, many believe that there is a fundamental flaw in the reporting system between the exchanges and the IRS and that virtually every employer is going to see penalty assessments that are incorrect. Of course it is impossible to predict this with any certainty, but based on what we are seeing, it is a likely possibility.

If and when you are audited, your systems and documentation will be key. For employers who are prepared, understand the law, have complied with the law and have meticulous documents to prove it, their audits should be quick and painless. It is those employers who do not think it is important to plan that are going to have painful audits. Not only can they expect the IRS to audit for ACA compliance, but we all know the federal government does not need much of an excuse to get access to as much of your information as possible.

Here are just a few of the documents you should have prepared and in one place in order to make sure you are prepared for an audit:

(1) Payroll Records

(2) Evidence of Lookback/Stability Period or Monthly Measurement Period Calculations. Should be clear and easy to understand in a report.

(3) Written evidence of Measurement Period and FTE calculations.

(4) Proof of Insurance Exchange Notification.

(5) Plan Document. (This has always been a requirement but few have it. Because of the ACA, it is critical to have a Plan document beginning in 2014.)

(6) Employee Handbooks (especially important if you are trying to establish certain classes of employees or that you have a company policy of employing people part time).

(7) Proof that Employees have accepted or declined coverage.

(8) Written Strategic Plan outlining ACA compliance checklist.

(9) Proof of all correspondence with Employees regarding the ACA. You should have a formal system of communication about the ACA. Be prepared to show how you communicated and that you understand the law. This can help in the event of a Whistleblower claim.

(10) Clear documentation of all disciplinary action taken against employees. This will be important in the event of a Whistleblower action.

Because we are dealing with documents that may become part of a tax file, all employers should adopt a 7-year document retention policy.

ACTION STEPS

1. If you are a Large Employer, you must start running all of the scenarios and numbers. If you do not understand this, you should find someone to help you. In doing your analysis, you may find that it makes sense to offer coverage or not to offer coverage. Make sure that your advisor understands all aspects of your business (i.e. How would scheduling down to part-time affect employee morale or customer service).

2. If you are in a Controlled Group, be sure to talk to a good attorney or CPA about how to strategize in this area. It may be some time for some restructuring. Pay special attention to the pro rata allocation of the less 30 among members of the controlled group.

3. Get your plan in place to begin documenting when employees are offered coverage and have them sign something if they decline.

4. You should already be meeting with your insurance advisors to explore the best insurance products for you. Make sure insurance company warrants that the insurance coverage you provide offers Minimum Essential Coverage.

5. Train all of your Managers on the OSHA Whistleblower Rules. Document everything.

6. Document. Document. Document. Be ready for audits and insurance exchange inquiries. Collect all the necessary documents and keep them in one place. Write summaries of what you are doing and of every meeting you hold with your staff. Keep copies of letters and memos sent out.

7. Adopt a 7-year document retention policy. Keep electronic documents that are easy to access when the time comes.

Chapter 5:
S is for Strategy

By failing to prepare, you are preparing to fail.
~Benjamin Franklin

Now is the fun part. Until now, we have mostly been talking about compliance which is the necessary first step. We cannot start breaking the rules until we understand them. Once we understand the basics, then we start finding different ways to get where we want to go.

When I refer to 'breaking the rules,' I am not referring to breaking the law. I am referring to understanding the law so well that you are able to take advantage of the solutions most people will never see or are afraid to try. It is the difference between a person who forms an LLC and asks to be paid as a 1099 consultant vs. a person who prefers to be paid as a W2 employee. The W2 employee may think his way is safer because he does not understand how to form an LLC, does not understand the tax implications and does not have a CPA to help him. The 1099 consultant, however, knows that her way is no less safe and it is going to result in her keeping a lot more of her money. The 1099 consultant is not breaking the law. She is just breaking the rules that most people falsely believe to be true.

Here is another example of what I'm talking

about in the business and insurance world. Almost all very large companies (think Disney, Wal-Mart, Safeway) self-insure. They self insure because it is more cost effective, they have more control and they get tax benefits. Most smaller companies purchase traditional insurance because they believe it is 'safer.' I have even sat in meetings with insurance brokers who did not understand self-insurance and advised their clients that self-insurance is very dangerous and that they are safer buying traditional insurance.

The reality is that self-insurance, if structured properly, is not less safe than traditional insurance. Set up properly, self-insurance is just as safe as traditional insurance but allows businesses to keep more of their money and control their program. For example, if you are using traditional insurance and you have a bad year, your rates go up and often never come back down. The traditional insurance company has to keep plenty of reserves on hand 'just in case' you have another bad year but if in fact you don't have a bad year, you never get that money back. Not only that, when you are using traditional insurance, you are paying for your insurance company's profits, marketing, real estate, football stadiums, etc.

Companies who self insure know where all of their money is going. They don't have large sums of money unnecessarily set aside for no reason and decide how much exposure they are going to have (like how we choose our deductible when we purchase car insurance). Self-insured companies have a say in how claims are handled and they enjoy tax benefits that companies who purchase traditional insurance will never see. Self-insurance is like the person who chose to be paid through her LLC. It is not breaking the law, it is breaking the rules that most people believe to be true.

Below I am going to discuss several of the ACA strategies I have seen. This list is not exhaustive by a long shot because people are thinking of new ideas every day.

1. Self Directed Insurance Trust

This program is ideal for companies that have to insure many more employees because of the ACA than they did in the past. The Self-Directed Insurance Trust is a self-insurance strategy that combines self-funding with captive and trust law. It provides additional protections as compared to traditional self-funded programs because, among other things, each owner is protected from liability of other members. This program also provides financial planning opportunities for participants.

This program is advantageous for employers because it takes care of the employer's onerous documentation requirements and if followed as designed, ensures ACA compliance. This program is coupled with an ACA compliant insurance plan that is both "affordable" and "minimum value" (as defined by the ACA) and therefore satisfies both the $2,000 excise tax and the $3,000 excise tax.

Pros: One of the most innovative and comprehensive solutions I have seen. The structure handles all of a company's reporting and documentation as well so a business owner has peace of mind that it is prepared for an IRS audit.

Cons: The insurance covers basic preventative and wellness coupled with a bronze plan. Companies accustomed to providing very generous insurance to their employees may want more coverage.

2. Self-Insurance

In a self-insured plan, the employer assumes the financial risk for providing its employees' health benefits. Typically, the employer sets aside a fund to cover the costs of claims and pays the claims as they arise rather than paying a fixed premium to an insurance company. There are many ways to set up a self-insurance plan and most self-insurance plans include stop loss coverage which covers losses over a certain dollar amount.

Because of the ACA's increased regulation over traditional insurance, we are going to see a lot more companies self insuring in the coming years. As long as it is structured properly, self-insurance is the safest, most cost effective solution for businesses to manage their risk and to maintain control of their claims.

Pros: Customizable. Employer maintains control over reserves. Employer does not pre-pay for coverage. Governed by ERISA so does not have to worry about state regulations or taxes. Employer is free to choose its provider network.

Cons: If a self-insurance program is not structured properly or if it does not have proper stop loss coverage, self-insured losses could be catastrophic.

3. Skinny Plans

This is a plan that only offers minimum essential coverage (MEC) and typically covers only preventative and wellness. A MEC plan is neither affordable nor does it provide minimum value. A MEC plan is designed to satisfy the $2,000 per employee per month penalty which is assessed if a large employer fails to offer coverage and one employee receives a subsidy on the exchange. Typically, a business owner will purchase the skinny plan for every full-time employee in the company. The problem is that skinny plans do not satisfy the $3,000 per employee per month penalty which is assessed if a large employer offers coverage but it is not affordable or minimum value.

Pros: Satisfies an employee's individual mandate to have health insurance. It is a low cost solution for employers.

Cons: Once an employee receives the MEC plan, he can still qualify for a subsidy on the exchange and therefore, this strategy leaves employers exposed to the $3,000 per employee per month penalty.

4. High Deductible Bronze Plans

In this strategy, employers offer their employees a bronze plan with high deductibles and co-pays with the hope that most employees will choose not to take it. The employers satisfy their employer mandate by "Offering" affordable, minimum value insurance to all of their full-time employees even though most of them do not take it. The biggest problem with this strategy is that most insurance companies have minimum participation requirements (e.g. at least 80% of your eligible employees must sign up in order to keep your quoted pricing).

I have seen many clients think this was a successful strategy and even be assured by their broker that there was no minimum participation requirements only to read the fine print later and find out they were mistaken. In one such instance, the employer fell far below the minimum participation requirements and the insurance company demanded the employer pay the difference. The employer and the insurance company are now in a legal battle over the contract the employer signed.

If you do in fact opt for this strategy, I recommend having your attorney review your contract to ensure there is nothing hidden in your contract with regard to minimum participation. Do not just rely on your broker's word. It is the contract that governs. Be aware that even if an insurance company agrees to a low participation plan the first year, this does not preclude them from raising your rates to make up for it in subsequent years.

Pros: If you can actually find an insurance company that will agree to do this, it could be a low cost solution.

Cons: Your employees who are offered this coverage and decline it become disqualified from receiving subsidies or cost sharing assistance on the insurance exchange. Also, if your employees have no options for affordable coverage (e.g. Medicaid or Medicare), they will still be on the hook for the Individual Mandate and will be assessed a penalty. In short, it actually costs your employee money to work for you.

5. Traditional Insurance

In a traditional full-insured plan, your company pays a premium to an insurance company. The premium rate is fixed for the year and you pay a monthly payment based on the number of employees enrolled in your plan. If the number of employees in the plan changes, the monthly payment could change. Typically the individuals covered under such a plan pay co-pays and deductibles related to their policy.

Traditional insurance is what most people are

used to so it feels safer and more predictable.

Pros: Safe. It is what most people are used to. Numerous plans to choose from with a great many options. You simply pay your premium and the insurance company handles everything. If cash-flow is an issue, traditional insurance may be the most viable option.

Cons: No control over claims or reserves. Insurance costs are going up as a result of the ACA. Governed by state insurance laws. Premiums are tax deductible but no other tax benefits (as compared to self-insurance). No transparency about where your money is going. Subject to network chosen by insurance company.

6. Private Exchanges

A private exchange is basically a private business operated by brokers or insurers that sells insurance to individuals and business through a website. It is unique because it allows individuals to shop from an array of different medical plans and supplemental products (e.g. dental, vision, life). The idea is similar to the federal insurance marketplace in that people enrolling in the insurance will go to the website, enter their information and see all of the plans for which they are qualified. Employers who use a private exchange for their employees also receive administrative services from the operators of the private exchange.

Employers can fund their employees' participation in their private exchanges through pre-tax income in the same way employers fund and subsidize traditional insurance plans. Typically private exchanges are funded in part with the use of "defined contributions." This is similar to a 401(k) retirement plan where employers contribute set amounts of money toward the employee's health insurance. Employees then choose their plan from the private exchange with the money allocated to them.

Private exchange companies have come a long way in structuring these complex arrangements. The real challenge will be structuring the insurance offerings in a way that satisfies the requirements under the employer mandate.

Pros: Gives employees options to choose from. The private exchange company handles all of the administration. Employers define the amount they are going to spend per employee. The competition of numerous insurance companies could keep employers' costs down.

Cons: Complexity in determining the right level of contribution for different employees and still be compliant under the ACA. Ensuring the structure of the plans being offered satisfies the ACA and does not leave employers exposed to the ACA penalties.

Nondiscrimination rules.

7. Pay the Penalty

In some instances, companies are opting to pay the penalty rather than offer insurance. The thing to keep in mind here is that the penalty (excise tax) is not tax deductible while paying for insurance is. Also the excise tax is a tax on money that is already subject to taxation so in the end it ends up being more than the $2,000 per employee per month or the $3,000 per employee per month written in the code.

There are two situations where an employer might opt to pay the penalty. First, an employer might opt to pay the $2,000 penalty for not offering coverage. Second, an employer might opt to pay the $3,000 penalty for offering coverage that not minimum value or affordable.

The first option almost never makes sense. For example, if you only have 51 full-time employees, you have to offer insurance to 95% of them. However, when calculating your "A" penalties you get to deduct the first 30. This means roughly that you will only be assessed a penalty with regard to 21 employees (after you deduct the first 30). If just one of those employees receives a subsidy on the exchange, you will be assessed a non tax deductible penalty of $42,000. The reason I say it almost never makes sense is that there are many insurance programs available that cost less than $2,000 per month and will be tax deductible to the employer.

The second option might make sense in limited circumstances. In the second option, the employer offers insurance to everyone, but the insurance might not be affordable and minimum value to everyone. In this scenario, the employer has satisfied the $2,000 penalty and is only exposed to the $3,000 penalty. The $3,000 penalty is only assessed for the employees that receive a subsidy (as opposed to the $2,000 penalty that is assessed for all full-time employees whether or not you are offering them insurance). Therefore, the employer might purposely choose to make the insurance affordable and minimum value to all but a select number of employees for which the employer opts to risk paying a penalty.

The idea here is that some employers believe that some employees will not pay for insurance on the exchange, even if it is subsidized. If they are right and the employees do not go to the exchange, the penalties will never be triggered. This is a very gutsy bet to make given the generous subsidies that are available. Also, when a family is dealing with an illness or a pregnancy, it is very likely that they will go to the exchange. When you consider that there are tax-deductible insurance plans available that cost less than the penalties, it rarely makes sense to pay an exorbitant excise tax.

Pros: Your employees will be free to qualify for a subsidy or cost sharing assistance on the exchange if you are not offering any insurance at all. There is a chance that none of your employees qualify for a subsidy on the exchange and no penalties ever get triggered.

Cons: Insurance premiums are tax deductible. Excise taxes are not. The excise taxes are taxed on income that is already subject to taxation so it ends up being more than you think it will be. Your employees will be subject to the penalties for not satisfying the individual mandate. You could pay far more than you would have if you had purchased insurance. If you are betting on employees not going to the exchange, you could lose that bet.

~

Why Plan Now?

My daughter was 5 years old when she first started playing tennis. Back then, it was a miracle if she even made contact between the tennis racket and the ball. After some time, her game started to improve, the number of times she made contact with the ball increased and her scurried movements around the court started to resemble the game of tennis. After 7 years of practice, she now has the requisite skill to be able to serve, keep score and play a full game with her instructor. Now is when the game gets really fun and she is learning how she can change her entire game with a slight tilt of her racket, an adjustment in the way she is holding it or how she is moving her feet.

This is what is happening with my clients. The ones who are educating themselves, who are working with me and who are getting prepared, are at a point now where they are fine-tuning their game. They already understand the basics of the law and have implemented a plan. When the new ACA changes come out, these folks only need to make minor adjustments and are not sent into a frenzy of confusion. Instead, they are perfectly positioned to start strategizing around their implementation strategy.

For those who have already started planning and understand the basics, their fear has abated. They are now sitting back and watching the political hysteria. They are also waiting to steal the market share from the employers who think they have plenty of time to plan, think the law is going to go away or who simply have their heads buried in the sand.

Planning Strategies

- **Your Internal Team.** It is important to make sure your HR and Payroll departments are well educated about the mandates. Likewise, if you are scheduling your staff to part-time, it is important that your managers understand why you are doing it and that they are following through. Who else in your organization needs to understand the requirements? Which department is responsible for tracking during the Look-Back

Period? The law is confusing. Is your staff getting the support and resources they need to learn it?

- **Established Business Policies and Procedures**. There is no quicker way to land yourself into hot water than to make sweeping changes in your company's hiring practices (i.e. scheduling everyone down to part time) and announce that you are doing it to avoid having to pay for health insurance. That is a textbook ERISA violation and an employment litigator will be serving you with a complaint in the next few months or years if you aren't careful. It is very important that you consult with an employment lawyer or HR specialist when you are instituting these policies to make sure you are not inadvertently getting yourself in trouble.

- **Your Outside Advisors.** Make sure that you are choosing outside advisors who have done their homework. The law is so new and still changing that there are not many 'experts' yet. However, there are many professionals out there who are well-versed on the Law. You will likely need to consult with a good CPA, an attorney, an insurance broker and possibly an HR consultant.

- **Strategic Plan.** Because there are so many moving parts and so many possible scenarios, it is critical for companies to create and implement a documented strategic plan. The strategic plan should be clear and concise and should be communicated to each department integral to carrying it out. The purpose of this is to make sure everyone is on the same page. There would be nothing worse than finding out too late that the department responsible for record keeping did not understand their importance to the overall plan.

- **Implementation Plan.** Just as important as the Strategic Plan, is the plan for carrying it out. Who in your organization is going to be charged with the different tasks ahead? Are you going to appoint one person to oversee everything? Where will documents be managed? Have you had your implementation plan reviewed by your tax attorney or CPA to make sure you are not missing anything?

- **Communication.** We have all seen news reports of tempers flaring because of poor communication over health care reform. If you are scheduling your employees to part-time, how are you communicating this change to them? Are you going to do it in such a way that creates anxiety and a bitter work force (not to mention an onslaught of worker's comp claims) or are you going to do it in a way that educates them and supports workplace morale? If you are changing your insurance plans, how is that being presented to your employees? Are you explaining it in a way that brings you good results for your organization or in a way that causes even more problems?

- **Put It In Writing**. Start a file and a physical binder where you print and keep documentation about your strategic plan and implementation plan. Write up a summary of what you did and why. It does not even need to be complete sentences (however, that would be ideal). The important thing is that you have documentation that you can show to the IRS two years after you are assessed penalties to show why you did what you did. Summarize every meeting, print it and put it in the binder. Print every letter and put it in the binder. The more that you can show that you made a good faith effort to comply with the law and that you were actually following a compliance strategy, the better it will be for you.

- **Electronic Data And Cloud Storage.** I recently walked into a client's office and he had 4 years of documents stored in physical boxes. Nothing was electronic. Since the only way to fight an assessment is through documentation up to 2 years after the fact, this is a recipe for disaster. If you have not already begun keeping electronic documents, this is the time to start. You not only want things to be physically accessible, you need to make sure that they are saved in ways that you can easily find what you are looking for. Since these documents could now become part of someone's permanent tax file, it is imperative that you not only store the information for 7 years but also that you store it securely. There are numerous inexpensive secure, unlimited cloud based storage solutions for business owners

Workforce Strategies

- **Scheduling workforce to Part-time.**
  - If you did not already start, this ship may have sailed. In the February 2014 guidance from the IRS, we were told that any effort to reduce your workforce to avoid the employer mandate will be ignored. Instead, workforce reductions will only be recognized if it was done for legitimate business purpose such as downsizing, marketplace economics, etc.
  - Many quick serve restaurants are using this as a strategy right now. It is important to explore if this is right for your business model. How will it impact customer service? Employee morale?
  - What benefit will be gained and at what cost? We anticipate that many full time employees may decline coverage in the first year, which means that if you offer coverage, you may not end up paying as much as you expected anyway. On the other hand, as individual penalties go up in coming years, we may see this change.
  - It is likely litigators are going to bring ERISA violation claims against employers who reduce hours in a clear attempt to avoid paying

benefits. If you do it, make sure that you can establish through your hiring policies and procedures and employee handbooks that you do this for a legitimate business purpose.

- As I mentioned above, if you have not begun this strategy already, you may have missed your opportunity.

- **Outsourcing**
  - Even if you lease your employees, the IRS is going to use the 'common-law employee' definition. If you control and direct the employee, he is considered your common law employee whether or not you are going through a staffing or leasing company.
  - The anti-abuse rules do not allow temporary staffing agencies, leasing companies or the employers who use them to avoid the mandate. If you do use an employee leasing company, you need to make sure that (1) the leasing company is offering the employee insurance and (2) that you are paying a fee for such employees that is higher than you would otherwise pay in order to cover the cost of the insurance. If you don't do this and the staffing company does not offer the employee insurance, you are the one who could be assessed a penalty.
  - If you are the staffing or employee leasing company, do not read my analysis to mean that you won't also be assessed a penalty. You will. Both you and the employer who utilizes your services meet the definition of common law employer. Therefore, both of

you are responsible for satisfying the employer mandate.

Pricing And Planning Strategies

- **Spousal Coverage:** Employers are not required to offer insurance to spouses of employees, and if you do offer coverage to spouses you are not required to contribute toward the cost. If cost is an issue, this may be something to consider. Also, if you do not offer spousal coverage, spouses may qualify for subsidies on the exchange. If you offer spouses coverage, even if that coverage is not affordable, the spouse will be ineligible to receive a subsidy on the exchange.

- **Dependent Coverage:** Employers are required to offer insurance to dependents beginning in 2015, but there is no requirement that the coverage be affordable. That means employers may require dependents to pay for 100% of the cost of their insurance.

- **Ninety Day Waiting Period:** Impose a 90-day waiting period before full-time employees can begin receiving insurance. If you have a business with high turnover, this waiting period may reduce the number of employees you have to offer coverage. (*In California, the waiting period for traditional insurance plans is 60 days*).

- **Measurement Periods:** These should be selected strategically. Most if not all employers are being advised to use a 12-month measurement period. If you have seasonal workers, you should use a 12-month measurement period because many of your seasonal workers will already be gone by the end of the period and you will not be required to offer them coverage.

Annual Reporting Requirements

- IRC §6056 and 6055: All applicable large employers, whether fully-insured or self-insured, will be required to file annual reports with the IRS.

- Form 1094-C: Employer Transmittal. This is the form employers will file with the IRS which will assist the IRS in determining if the employer will be assessed excise taxes for failure to offer minimum essential, affordable coverage to their employees.

- Form 1095-C: Employee Statement. This is the form employers must be furnished to employees before January 31 of the year following the year to which it relates.

ACTION STEPS

1. Devise a Strategic Plan and an Implementation Plan. Get buy-in from your team and make sure you know who is responsible for executing the plan.

2. Put it in writing. It does not need to be well-written or done by an attorney. Just write out what you did and why.

3. Start storing your documentation electronically.

4. Find the right advisors. All advisors are not created equal. Find professionals who have studied the law and are aware of best practices.

5. Educate yourself and your employees. The law is confusing and it is changing frequently. Be sure that your organization is equipped with the most up to date information. Share best practices with other business owners.

6. Begin communicating with your employees about what is ahead. If you are going to change policies (i.e. become a part-time employer) be sure to consult with an employment attorney or HR specialist so you can avoid creating liability for yourself.

7. Start brainstorming and planning with your insurance broker on pricing and planning strategies.
8. If you are a Large Employer, explore alternative insurance strategies (i.e., Self-Insurance, Private Exchanges, Skinny Plans, etc.)

9. Understand annual reporting requirements and begin working with your CPA to be prepared.

Chapter 6:
Go Forth and Conquer

Take time to deliberate, but when the time for action comes, stop thinking and go in.
~ Napoleon Bonaparte

As you can see by now, my approach to Obamacare implementation is unique. I am not telling you to spend hours learning every detail of the law. I am also not telling you to hire a consultant to do it for you. I am advocating that you learn the down and dirty basics of the law so that you can start thinking strategically. When you understand the overall context of the law and how it will impact your business, you will be better equipped to know when and where to go for help.

The law is still evolving and I cannot anticipate what it is going to look like in 6 months or a year from now. Naturally, this uncertainty is going to breed fear. One hundred percent of the time, my clients were much more fearful before they were armed with the facts and much calmer after they had a plan of attack. My goal is to help bring certainty when possible and to help devise a strategy when it is not.

Recommendations:

- **Seek Answers And Stay Tuned To Changes.** You may think you understand the Law today but new guidance could come out tomorrow that could drastically change it.

- **Keep An Open Mind**. If you approach this through a lens – any lens – then there are things you will not see. If you approach it with an open mind you will see things you did not even know you did not know. There are opportunities to plan and strategize. However, if you are stuck in believing you have the answers or in believing that there are no answers, you will limit what is possible for you.

  One good example is traditional insurance. Most employers in this country are used to purchasing traditional insurance. However, the increasing demands on insurance companies as a result of the ACA are requiring savvy business owners to look into alternatives, such as self-insurance and captives. Very large companies have been using these strategies for years, but it is only recently that mid-sized companies have begun getting involved. The tax savings alone can in some instances fund a company's entire ACA implementation strategy.

- **Take Action**. If you have been paralyzed with information overload up to now… knock it off. It is time to dive in and start swimming.

  Think about how much worse a task is when you procrastinate. When we finally force ourselves to get it done, it is never as bad as we thought it would be and we are relieved that it is finally finished. The ACA is challenging, but not nearly as challenging as most people think.

- **Put It In Writing**. Document everything you are doing and save it in a format that will be easy to find 2 to 3 years down the road.

- **Who Is On Your Team**? Have you found a Lawyer and CPA who understand the ACA? Does your insurance broker understand the law? What about an HR advisor? It takes every one of these disciplines to navigate these waters. If you have not found them yet, find them.

- **Make A Plan**. I won't hold you to it. Just make one. You can always revise it as you go.

- **Resources.** Too much information out there? I agree. Find a few trusted sources that are providing you with regular legislative updates.

- **Keep It Simple**. Any time things are feeling too complicated or confusing, there is always another way. You do not have to understand every detail of the law. Learn the big picture and learn where to go for help.

A SILVER LINING?

It is a little known fact that more millionaires are created during times of economic political crisis than in any other time in our country's history. How can that be? Well, it is obviously not because of the economic crisis. That would be counter-intuitive.

The reason for this phenomenon is because of the way these individuals choose to view their circumstances.

During economic and political crisis, some people merely react to their environment. They go into survival mode and often succumb to the suggestion that they will be negatively affected. Others are economically prepared to take advantage of the opportunities that arise. They have amassed wealth that allows them to buy low or have enough reserves to weather the storm. However, the ones who jump the curve and thrive in spite of the destruction are the ones who see opportunities and new ways of doing things where other people only see problems.

Citing numerous examples of companies who have modeled innovation and success, Guy Kawasaki explains how some companies 'jump the curve' by breaking old patterns of thinking and behavior. In Malcom Gladwell's book, the Tipping Point, he explains how one single decision or action can spark a trend that when it reaches 'critical mass' can spread like wildfire. In Good to Great, Jim Collins does an in-depth analysis of what makes companies succeed while others merely survive or fail. The "Great" companies are not the ones that had ideal political and environmental conditions. The "Great" companies are the ones who confront the brutal facts and never lose faith.

Here is a list of a few well-known companies that completely beat the odds and prospered in spite of a large-scale economic downturn:

- Disney, 1923-24, Recession.
- Hewlett-Packard, Great Depression.
- Xerox began in 1966, post World War I recession.
- Kellogg stole market share from Post during the Great Depression.
- Interstate Bakeries (Twinkies!) 1933
- Microsoft, recession of 1975
- CNN, USA Today, and MTV, economic slump of the early 80's
- Wikipedia, post 911 recession
- Google, PayPal and Salesforce.com, 2000-2004

If they can do it, anyone can do it. These companies did not change their environment overnight. They changed the way they viewed their environment and their experience within it changed. We either look at everything as if it is an opportunity or as if nothing is.

I have given it to you straight. The Affordable Care Act is one of the most frustrating and confusing laws for employers I have seen during my career. However, while the media and Facebook politicians are forecasting doom and gloom, I have been busy looking for solutions and opportunities.

There are solutions here. There are also opportunities here. I work with a number of think tanks and companies who are finding innovative ways to deal with the ACA. In this book I have even told numerous stories of employer who have found ways to turn implementing the ACA into profit centers.

The bottom line is that there is no more time and no more excuses to delay. The time to plan is now. What you do this year will directly impact your obligations and penalties in the next few years. Ideally, you get the basics down quickly so you can start thinking strategically and hopefully you, too, can figure out how to turn implementing Obamacare into a profit center for your company.

Your Obamacare Advisors (YOA) is a resource and think tank on all things Obamacare. YOA is a team of professionals who help companies create strategic plans and take concrete action steps to implement Obamacare in their organizations. The YOA Team is committed to providing up to date information to their clients and monitoring changes so that their clients can focus on their businesses.

www.YourObamacareAdvisors.com

info@YourObamacareAdvisors.com.

APPENDIX A

Verification of Insurance Status

Section 1: Employee Information

Name: ______________________________

Address: ______________________________

SSN: ______________________________

Date of Birth: ___/___/______

[ ] Spanish is employee's primary language.

Classification:

[ ] Variable Hour [ ] Salary [ ] Eligible Dependent of Employee

Job Title: ______________________________

Section 2: Employer Information

Employer: ______________________________

Cell Number: ______________________________

Plan Type: ______________________________

Section 3: Enrollment Eligibility Information

[ ] New Employee Date of Hire/Full Time: ___/___/______

[ ] Open Enrollment Date of Event: ___/___/______

[ ] Loss of Other Medical Coverage Date of Event ___/___/______

[ ] Marriage Date of Event: ___/___/______

[ ] New Dependent Child Date of Event: ___/___/______

[ ] Court Order Date of Event:

Section 4: Election of Coverage

[ ] I am **accepting** the employer sponsored health insurance[10] that is being offered by my employer. I understand that my contribution toward the health insurance plan offered by my employer will be deducted from my pay and will not exceed 9.5% of my income.

Section 5: Waiver of Coverage

[ ] I have been offered employer sponsored health insurance from my employer, but I have **WAIVED** acceptance. I understand that I am not qualified to receive subsidized insurance on my state's health insurance exchange by waiving Qualified and Affordable employer-sponsored Minimum Essential Coverage. I understand that if I apply for insurance on my state's health insurance exchange, I must respond under penalty of perjury that I have been offered Qualified and Affordable Minimum Essential Coverage by my employer. I also understand that unless I qualify for health insurance from another source or an exemption, I may be subject to a penalty for failure to comply with the Individual Mandate[11].

Section 6: Signature of Employee

By signing below, I verify that all information I have provided in this Verification of Insurance Status is accurate to the best of my knowledge. I have read and understood

---

[10] Note: By "health insurance," this document intends the reader to interpret this as "minimum essential coverage" as defined by IRC § 4980H(a).

[11] Note: Individual Mandate and timing by which to meet this mandate subject to certain limited exceptions as noted in PPACA.

this Verification of Insurance Status and understand that I may not change a waiver of coverage under Section 5 until the next enrollment period on my employer's plan or occurrence of a subsequent qualified event as noted in the Summary Plan Description.

Coverage may be amended or rescission may occur if employee provides knowingly false, misleading, or incomplete information on this form.

Signature: ___________________________________

Printed Name: _______________________________

Date: ___/___/______

APPENDIX B

Employee Notice: Your Health Care Options for 2014

As your employer, [Company Name] is always striving to maintain a welcoming, inspiring, and beneficial atmosphere for you and your family. Together, we work to create a great experience for our clients and our employees. Your hard work has helped us grow as a company and as a positive local impact on your community and others.

Over the past few years, you may have heard about a new law concerning your health care. It has many names, such as the Patient Protection and Affordable Care Act, health care reform, and even "Obamacare." This new law has affected health plans already, but this October it will directly affect you and your family.

To keep you up to date on these important changes, [Company Name] has put together this brochure to inform you of what your options for health care will look like under the new health care reform law in 2014 and beyond.

The Individual Mandate

Under the new law, all individuals must have health insurance beginning January 1, 2014.[12] This means that you and your family must have health insurance, or you will be penalized with an extra tax. This 2014 tax penalty is either $95 per adult plus $47.50 per minor, or 1% of your household income, whichever is greater. The maximum penalty you may owe is **three times the regular penalty**

[12] Note: Individual Mandate and timing by which to meet this mandate subject to certain limited exceptions as noted in PPACA.

amount. Some examples to help you understand how this penalty could affect you are below.

Family Type	Penalty Amount
You	$95 or 1% of your household income for the year
You and Your Spouse	$190 or 1% household income
You and Your Minor Child	$142.50 or 1% household income
You, Spouse, and 1 Minor Child	$237.50 or 1% household income
Maximum Penalty Per Family	$285 or 1% household income

Remember, you will either pay the dollar amount shown or the percentage of your household income. You will pay the greater amount. **You will only owe this penalty if you do not have health insurance in 2014.**[13]

Information on the New Health Insurance Exchanges
Beginning October 1, 2013, some states and the federal government will open a new way to buy health insurance, known as a **Health Insurance Marketplace**, also known

[13] Note: By "health insurance," this document intends the reader to interpret this as "minimum essential coverage" as defined by IRC § 4980H(a).

as the health insurance exchange, state exchange, or federal exchange.

Before we discuss the marketplace, we must note that you have alternatives to exchange plans. Your first option is the new **[Company name] Plan** that you are eligible for. Other plans you can choose from include **Medicaid**, **Medicare**, the **Children's Health Insurance Program**, your **spouse's plan**, your **parent's plan** if you are under the age of 26, or an **individual plan** you obtain from an insurance company on your own. All of these options satisfy the individual mandate.

The marketplace can help you find options that meet your needs and fit your budget. Open enrollment for health insurance coverage offered by the Marketplace begins October 1, 2013, and coverage starts as early as January 1, 2014.[14]

By applying for an exchange plan and meeting certain criteria, you may qualify for tax credits to assist in paying for the exchange plan. You may be wondering how to qualify for a tax credit if you decide to look at an exchange plan. Eligibility depends on two requirements, discussed below.

First, you have to earn within certain amounts of income to qualify. This amount is different depending on how big your family is, so even if you earn the same amount as your colleagues, those employees with bigger families may satisfy this requirement when you alone do not.

---

[14] Note: These dates subject to change by the controlling exchange.

Second, you can only receive this tax credit if [Company Name] does not offer a certain type of health plan to you, known under the law as an affordable, minimum value plan. [Company Name], due to the federal government's mandate, must provide this plan or face negative consequences.

As a result, the [Company Name] Plan [will/will not/may] provide you affordable, minimum value coverage. One of the side effects of affordable, minimum value plan is that you will not qualify for aid on an exchange plan. However, an offer of affordable, minimum value coverage does **not** mean that you will not be able to access exchange plan benefits, if you want them. You may still enroll in an exchange plan, but no tax credits will be available.

We must note that affordability means the plan does not cost you more than 9.5% of your monthly adjusted gross income, and minimum value means at least 60% of the actuarial value of the plan is covered by the employer.

Note: If you purchase a health plan through the marketplace instead of accepting health coverage offered by [Company Name], then you may lose the employer contribution (if any) to the employer-offered coverage. This employer contribution, along with your employee contribution to employer-offered coverage, is often excluded from income for federal and state income tax purposes. Your payments for coverage through the marketplace are made on an after-tax basis.

If you still have questions about the marketplace, please

visit www.Healthcare.gov for more information, including an online application for health insurance coverage and contact information for a health insurance marketplace in your area. If you have questions about your new health plan options or the marketplace, please contact us through the following information:

[Company Name]; [Company Address]; [Company Phone #]
Point of Contact: [Company Name HR Point of Contact]
[Company Name HR Point of Contact #]
[Company Name Web Site]; [Company Name HR Point of Contact Email]

This document functions as a Notice of State Exchanges and Employer Plan Options, as mandated by PPACA § 1512 and FLSA § 18B. Any statements concerning health plan options for a plan year beginning on or after January 1, 2015 is subject to change. This document is intended as educational material for employees and dependents of said employees of [Company Name]. This document does not nor does it intend to create any contract for employment with any party. This document does not intend to make a promise of any health benefits to employees and their dependents. This document intends to comply with all pertinent federal law. Any conflict between federal law and this document should be construed such that federal law (or any relevant controlling law) overrides this document to the extent of such noncompliance. This document is not intended for viewing by any party other than an employee or dependent of [Company Name]. If this document was received in error by another party, please return or dispose of this document.

ABOUT THE AUTHOR

Kaya Bromley is an attorney, speaker, author and recognized business strategist. She is the founder and CEO of Your Obamacare Advisors (YOA) and has been recognized for her work in developing FreedomCare Benefits, a state of the art, Affordable Care Act (ACA) compliant program for large employers. Kaya's first book, "The Obamacare Roadmap" was originally published in 2013 to critical acclaim.

Kaya is currently a trustee of California's largest restaurant workers comp self-insured group and is an owner of two Tropical Smoothie Cafés located in Michigan. Previously, Kaya served as General Counsel for the Marco's Pizza Franchise and as the Executive Director of the National Jack-in-the-Box Franchisee Association. The businesses Kaya has advised on the ACA include insurance companies, brokers, farm labor contractors, payroll companies as well as franchisees of McDonald's, Burger King, El Pollo Loco, Five Guys and Carl's Jr. Kaya's gift of simplifying complex concepts has assisted hundreds of organizations in designing and implementing individualized strategic plans for the ACA.

Kaya is a second-generation entrepreneur and Detroit-area native, where she continues to hold an equity position in a for-profit dental supply business. She is also an inventor who has a patent in a hands-free teeth-whitening product. Kaya earned her undergraduate and masters degrees from Wayne State University in Detroit, before graduating with honors from Michigan State University Law School. She currently lives with her husband and daughter in the Lake Tahoe/Reno area of Nevada and maintains strong business ties in the San Francisco Bay area.

Made in the USA
Lexington, KY
12 April 2016